Italy's Three Crowns

Reading Dante, Petrarch and Boccaccio

Italy's Three Crowns
Reading Dante, Petrarch and Boccaccio

Edited by

Zygmunt G. Barański and Martin McLaughlin

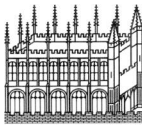

Bodleian Library
UNIVERSITY OF OXFORD

Credits

Figures 1-10, 12, 14-34, 36, 38-43, 48-49 © Bodleian Library, University of Oxford

Figures 11 and 13 reproduced by permission of the Rector and Fellows of Exeter College, Oxford

Figures 35, 37 and 44 © Taylor Institution Library, University of Oxford

Figures 45 and 47 © Ashmolean Museum, Oxford. Reproduced by permission of the Ashmolean Museum, Oxford

Figure 46 © Tate Enterprises Ltd. Reproduced by permission of Tate Images

Figure 48 reproduced by permission of Oxford University Press

Figures 50-57 © Tom Phillips. Reproduced by kind permission of Tom Phillips

Cover: *The Tuscan Poets* by the School of Vasari, reproduced by kind permission of the Provost and Fellows of Oriel College, Oxford. Photograph © Nick Pollard

First published in 2007 by the Bodleian Library
Broad Street
Oxford OX1 3BG
www.bodleianbookshop.co.uk

ISBN: 1 85124 301 1
ISBN 13: 978 1 85124 301 3

Text © the contributors
Images © Bodleian Library, University of Oxford, and other named copyright holders, 2007
All rights reserved

Designed by Dot Little
Printed and bound by The University Press, Cambridge
British Library Catalogue in Publishing Data
A CIP record of this publication is available from the British Library

This book is published to accompany the exhibition *Italy's Three Crowns*, held at the Bodleian Library from 19 June to 31 October 2007.

Contents

Introduction

Zygmunt G. Barański and Martin McLaughlin

The essays in this volume have a double focus. On the one hand, they explore aspects of how Italy's three greatest writers, called the *Tre Corone* or Three Crowns – Dante, Petrarch, and Boccaccio – were received in the late Middle Ages and the Renaissance. On the other, they document the extraordinary revival of British interest in Dante during the last two hundred years – the other two writers never achieved a similar return to prominence – after the waning of the poet's reputation in the seventeenth and eighteenth centuries.

The first four chapters survey the significance of the Three Crowns for Italian culture up to the Renaissance. Zygmunt Barański (chapter 1) and Simon Gilson (chapter 4) trace the history of Dante's reception in Italy from the beginning of the fourteenth to the end of the sixteenth century. They highlight the ways in which the author of the *Commedia* exerted a sway over all aspects of Italian life, from the university classroom to the pulpit, and from the workshops of book producers to the street. More than anyone else, Dante became associated with a range of artistic, cultural, linguistic, and ideological issues which no intellectual could afford to ignore.

Martin McLaughlin (chapter 2) and Christopher Stevens (chapter 3) examine how Petrarch and Boccaccio dealt with Dante's legacy even as they forged new paths of their own. For if Dante inaugurated a cultural and linguistic revolution by writing his epic poem in the vernacular, Petrarch set in motion a counter-revolution which reinstated Latin as the superior language. Petrarch's humanism, and his re-discovery of the texts and values of classical antiquity, started an intellectual fashion that – when blended with other vernacular traditions – led to the efflorescence of literature and the arts in Italy known as the Renaissance. In fact both Petrarch and Boccaccio also wrote major works in Italian that incorporated some of the high cultural values of the ancient world. The visual interpretations of their works, as of Dante's, are rich and varied; and some of the manuscripts and early printed editions of the two writers, particularly of Boccaccio, reveal a microcosm of Italian Renaissance art.

The final four chapters concentrate on the role played by scholars and artists working in Britain, and especially some of those associated with Oxford, in reviving Dante's reputation. Taking the figure of Francesca da Rimini, Alex MacMillan (chapter 5) shows how, as the Romantic movement developed, Dante's themes became involved with some of the nineteenth century's most vital artistic and ideological concerns: interpretations ranged from a sentimental, to a political, to an aestheticized Francesca. John Woodhouse (chapter 6) charts the impact the Rossetti family had on the dissemination of Dante within British culture. Gabriele Rossetti wrote arcane commentaries on Dante's work, seeing him as a kind of proto-Mason, using a coded language to denounce the Church. His much better-known son, Dante Gabriel Rossetti, was responsible for a more aesthetic diffusion of the cult of Dante, through his sensitive translations and in his influential paintings. Diego Zancani (chapter 7) reviews the work of the foremost British Dante scholar of the late nineteenth and early twentieth centuries, Paget Toynbee. He was a major collector of manuscripts and early editions of the *Tre Corone*, but he also made key contributions to the philological study of the *Commedia* and compiled the first Dante dictionary. The volume concludes with artist Tom Phillips reflecting on the genesis of his own visualization of the *Commedia* and how this fits into the centuries-old tradition of Dante illustration and scholarship.

Given the complex influence of Italy's Three Crowns on Western culture, this volume cannot aim to be exhaustive. However, by concentrating on the aspects of their reception studied here, it is possible to form an idea of these writers' impact, and to begin to clarify the reasons for their remarkable and lasting allure.

This book was written to coincide with the fifth International Dante Seminar ('Dante lirico e etico') held at Somerville College, Oxford, in September 2007, and with the exhibition on the *Tre Corone* at the Bodleian Library, 19 June to 31 October 2007. The editors wish to thank all the staff they have encountered at the Bodleian Library for their generous help and cooperation, in particular Bruce Barker-Benfield, Alan Coates, Samuel Fanous, Francesca Galligan, Colin Harris, Dana Josephson, Martin Kauffmann, Dot Little, Madeline Slaven, and Deborah Susman.

CHAPTER I

'Honour the loftiest poet': Dante's reception in fourteenth-century Italy

Zygmunt G. Barański

'Dante, a theologian, lacking no doctrine which philosophy may cherish in her illustrious breast, glory of the Muses, the best-loved author of the common people'; 'Dante Alighieri, a man of deep and renowned wisdom, a disciple of philosophy, and the loftiest poet'; 'Dante was … distinguished in his manners and well-versed in many sciences, and especially in the sciences of the poets … indeed no mortal can be compared to him in the glory of language.'[1] Today such assessments of Dante (1265–1321), with the exception of the claim regarding his popularity among ordinary people, would seem neither especially noteworthy nor excessive. For intellectuals in the fourteenth century, however, to be asserting as much about a contemporary, even one who belonged to their cultural and geographical milieu, was remarkable. More significantly, their reactions point to the fact that, by the early Trecento, a major cultural revolution was under way in the Italian peninsula.

Before Dante wrote the *Commedia* (1306/7–21), no post-classical author had been celebrated with such vigour and in such evocative and culturally loaded terms — especially not one who, in a world dominated by Latin, had 'scandalously' decided to write using his own native language. Indeed, the encomiastic language used to describe Dante had for centuries been applied almost exclusively to the great writers and thinkers of antiquity. Dante himself had been following convention when he presented Virgil, the poet of the *Aeneid*, being 'honoured' in Limbo as 'l'altissimo poeta' ('the loftiest poet', *Inf.* IV.80);[2] a few cantos later, Dante terms Virgil the 'courteous, all-knowing sage' (*Inf.* VII.3).

However, as far as some of Dante's fourteenth-century readers were concerned, the 'new poet' was not just on a par with but actually superior to his classical forebears. Although most were chary about aggressively asserting such a radical and disturbing view, it emerges time and again in their writings that this really was their opinion. For instance, the Carmelite friar Guido da Pisa (thirteenth–fourteenth centuries) first refers to Virgil conventionally

as the 'greatest poet', but then, immediately afterwards, declares that Dante 'must be judged so much greater than all the others, as he composed the greatly sublime work [the *Commedia*]'.[3]

Such obviously incompatible assessments could only undermine the traditional literary hierarchy and challenge established perceptions regarding the status of the poets of antiquity, thereby drawing attention to and augmenting Dante's burgeoning reputation (Fig. 1). Questions of authority (*auctoritas*) – namely, who should be deemed worthy to hold cultural, intellectual, artistic, and moral sway over the present and then, having been elevated to the rank of *auctor*, to serve as a model for others to imitate in the future – were at the core of the transformation that took place in fourteenth-century Italy. Authority controlled every area of medieval life, since, as Dante explained in the *Convivio* ('Banquet', 1303–6/7), '"authority" means the same as "an activity worthy of being trusted and obeyed"'.[4]

Dante's first readers, in fact, were following a trail carefully laid by the poet himself. When he first meets Virgil in *Inferno*, the wayfarer declares, 'You are the one from whom alone I took | the noble style that has brought me honour' (*Inf.* I.86–87). While praising Virgil, Dante thus cleverly established his own poetic credentials, and this at the very start of the *Commedia*. In the following canto, by having Virgil speak of Beatrice, Dante drew his readers' attention to the *Vita nova* ('New Life', 1292–94), the work on which, as he began to compose the *Commedia* around 1306/7, his reputation still largely rested. A further two cantos later, Dante presents himself as welcomed in Limbo by the great canonical poets of antiquity – Homer, Virgil, Horace,

Ovid, and Lucan – 'so that I became the sixth amidst such wisdom' (*Inf.* IV.102) (Fig. 2). In granting himself this exalted status – a status that no post-classical writer had previously achieved – Dante usurped the position held by Terence, the established authority on comedy. His new, contemporary, Christian, and vernacular 'comedía' (*Inf.* XVI.128 and XXI.2), building on his earlier achievements, was about to replace a centuries-old and highly respected tradition.

Nor was Dante making claims that he could not substantiate. The genius and uniqueness of his poetry immediately confirmed the truth of his assertions. With the *Commedia* Dante gave a tremendous boost of confidence and energy to the nascent vernacular culture. He proved that using one's own native language not only was not a bar to success, but also did not prevent one from addressing the most complex theological and doctrinal topics or from being artistically innovative. The *Commedia* heads in new and unexpected directions. Its rhyme scheme, carefully partitioned structure, linguistic and stylistic range, 'realism', and 'encyclopaedic' span are all unprecedented. Put simply, Dante demonstrated that the vernacular (or at any rate *his* vernacular) could match, and even surpass, anything that Latin had achieved. There were many in the Trecento who agreed with him and were willing to mark and consolidate his extraordinary attainment publicly.

The many fourteenth-century commentaries written to accompany the *Commedia* offer the clearest proof of this consensus. They are also the most important feature of the earliest reactions to the poet and his masterpiece. The commentaries were closely based on the established forms of Scriptural and classical exegesis. However, what fundamentally distinguished them from their models was that they focused their attention on a 'modern' text and author. The commentaries on the *Commedia* were not the first examples of formal exegesis of a non-classical work, or even of one composed in the vernacular. Guido Cavalcanti's (?1260–1300) notoriously difficult philosophical *canzone* 'Donna me prega' ('A lady asks me'), was probably glossed during Dante's lifetime; but such instances are both slight and extremely rare. No other post-classical text had come even close to generating the kind of sustained, programmed, and detailed commentary that Dante's poem inspired (Fig. 3; and see also Fig. 10). In the Middle Ages, there was no more significant recognition of an author's *auctoritas* than for his writings to be systematically explicated.

2.
Dante and the great canonical poets of classical antiquity (Venetian, late 14th century). Oxford, Bodleian Library, MS. Canon. Ital. 108, fol. 4r.

3.
The opening tercets of
the *Inferno* surrounded by
Benvenuto da Imola's Latin
commentary, here translated
into Italian (Venetian,
first half of 15th century).
Oxford, Bodleian Library,
MS. Canon. Ital. 107, fol. 2v.

The earliest extant commentary, written by Dante's son Jacopo (*c.*1300–48)
to the *Inferno*, can be dated to 1322, the year after the poet's death in Ravenna.
However, Dante enjoyed considerable recognition during his lifetime. For two
decades – especially after his exile from Florence in 1302, on false charges of
corruption levelled by his political enemies – Dante was Italy's best-known and
most influential writer and intellectual. The *Vita nova* had firmly established
his literary reputation, yet there is no doubt that Dante's *auctoritas* was largely
based on the *Commedia*. The history of the poet's reception in the Trecento is
primarily the history of his reception as the author of the 'sacred poem' (*Par.*
XXIII.62 and XXV.1), to such an extent that in Florence the *Commedia* became
known as 'il Dante'. The obsession with the *Commedia* also helps to explain
the limited circulation of Dante's other works in the fourteenth century. It is

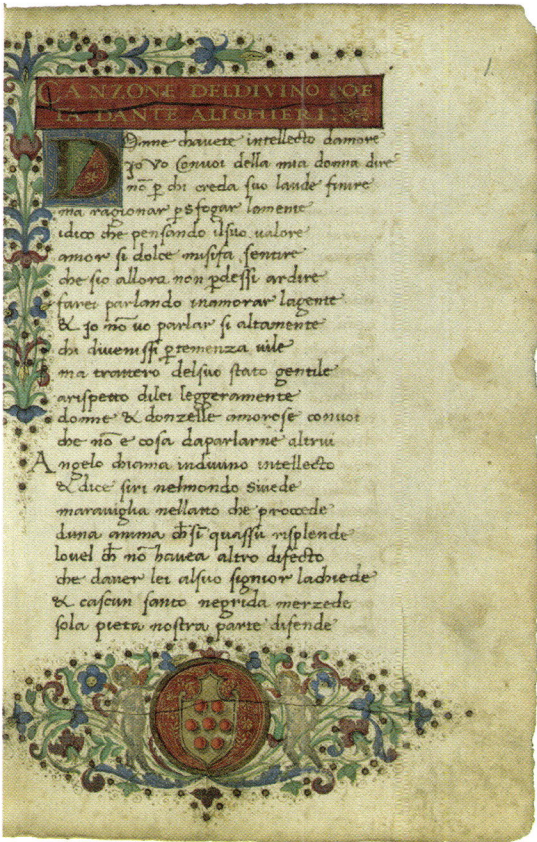

4.
A late fifteenth-century copy of Dante's famous canzone 'Donne ch avete intelletto d'amore', 'Ladies who have understanding of love'. Oxford, Bodleian Library, MS. Canon. Ital. 99, fol. 1r.

not until the Quattrocento, for instance, that his lyric production begins to be copied on a regular basis (Fig. 4).

The poem's first two canticles, *Inferno* and *Purgatorio*, and possibly batches of cantos of the third, *Paradiso*, began to circulate in Italy during the last decade or so of the poet's life. The success of the *Commedia* was immediate. Its prestige and uniqueness, together with those of its creator, were recognized in the many vernacular and Latin poems, powerfully celebratory in tone, written to mark Dante's death and to honour his authorship of the *Commedia*. The quotation that opened the present chapter was taken from the most famous of these, the Latin epitaph by the early humanist scholar Giovanni del Virgilio (late thirteenth century–*c*.1327).

The *Commedia* was the first work in the vernacular to reach the whole of the Italian peninsula. The poem's 'national' prominence is confirmed by the fact that commentaries to it were written in places as far apart as Milan, Naples, Pisa, and Verona, as well as in Dante's native Florence. Furthermore, as the manuscript evidence demonstrates, in fourteenth-century Italy the *Commedia* was the most popular book after the Bible. The manuscript tradition reveals that copies of the poem, ranging from richly illustrated codices (Fig. 5) to less ostentatious, relatively swiftly produced exemplars (Fig. 6), were made

for different audiences. In particular, to satisfy the demands of Florence's growing bourgeois-mercantile class, a flourishing market of quasi-serial production of the *Commedia* developed after 1350. The most famous copies of this kind originated from Francesco di ser Nardo da Barberino's workshop and have become known as 'the group of the One Hundred', referring to their supposed number. It was said that ser Nardo produced so many copies not simply to fulfil the orders of his fellow-citizens, but also because he had to find dowries for his several daughters.

The *Commedia*'s penetration into every part of the peninsula is all the more remarkable because the Florentine in which the poem is written would have been far from familiar to the majority of its readers. Medieval Italy's linguistic fragmentation into many distinct regional vernaculars was first recorded by Dante himself, in his *De vulgari eloquentia* ('On Vernacular Eloquence', 1304–6). Indeed, whatever their other aims, one of the primary functions of non-Tuscan commentaries especially was to make Dante's language accessible to readers in different regions. Commentators translated sections of the *Commedia* into Latin and offered detailed prose paraphrases and summaries of cantos (though the latter two features were typical of large-scale commentaries on the *auctores*). Equally, as the number of literate readers versed only in their native language grew, commentaries originally written in Latin were translated into the vernacular (Fig. 7). Given its extraordinary coverage, the poem's influence ranged from the schools to the pulpit and into the street. What is striking and unique about the first generations of the poem's readers and listeners is the diversity of their backgrounds and of their social origins. Thus, behind

Franco Sacchetti's (*c*.1332–1400) invented tales of blacksmiths incorrectly reciting verses from the *Commedia*, one can catch a glimpse of the degree to which Dante's masterpiece had quickly entered popular consciousness.[5]

However, despite the rapid growth in literacy during the Trecento (especially in Florence), it is almost certain that the *Commedia* was not actually read by the common people. Contemporary claims of Dante's appeal to the vulgar crowd were normally voiced by those who, whatever else they thought about the poet and his work, disapproved of his having written in the vernacular rather than in Latin, the sole language long deemed appropriate for intellectual endeavour. Giovanni del Virgilio's allusion to Dante's popularity therefore introduces a note of reproof into his epitaph's tone of sorrowful appreciation. A year or so earlier Giovanni had expressed the same reservation, in rather more vigorous terms, in a pair of Latin poems he had sent to the poet of the *Commedia*. As I discuss below, not all reactions to the poet and his poem were positive; nor is this remarkable, if one remembers the violent cultural shock caused by Dante.

The diversity of the *Commedia*'s audience partly accounts for the variety – in form, language, and content – of critical responses to the poem. In-depth, organically structured commentaries in Latin and in Italian ranged from analyses of all one hundred *canti* of the *Commedia* to interpretations of individual canticles or even of just a single canto. The poem together with its author inspired a plethora of other texts in both prose and verse. These include public lectures, summaries, pseudo-biographies, short stories, and discontinuous and connected glosses.[5] It goes without saying that no author since classical antiquity had generated such interest. As a further mark of respect and canonization, it was not unusual for different texts relating to Dante to be bound together in a single codex. An Oxford manuscript[7] contains, *inter*

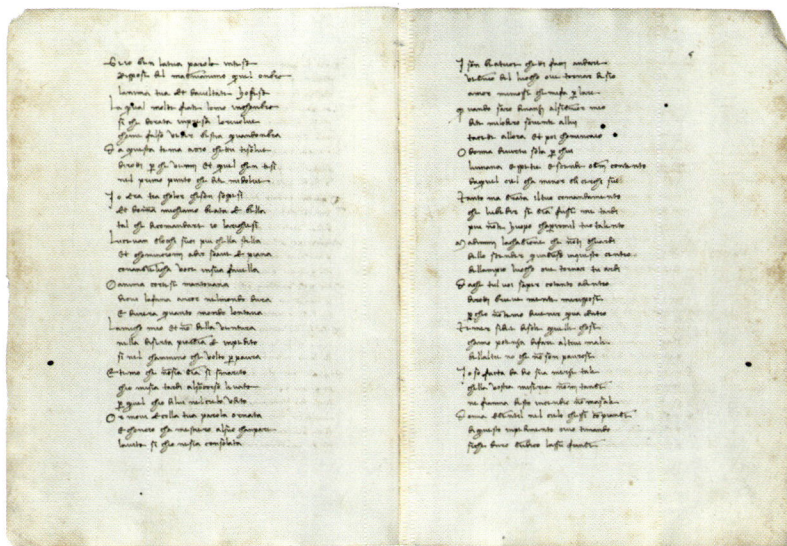

6.
Unillustrated copy of the *Commedia* with rubricated initials (*Inferno* II and III) (Tuscan, 15th century). Oxford, Bodleian Library, MS. Canon. Ital. 95 fols. 4v–5r.

a gloria di coluy che tuto moue
per luniuerso penetra e rissplende
Jn una parte piu e meno altroue.

alia, the prologues of several commentaries, Alberico da Rosciate's (*c.*1290–1360) commentary to the *Paradiso*, a Latin translation of Jacopo della Lana's commentary to the *Inferno*, and the complementary introductory poems to the *Commedia* by Bosone da Gubbio (1262/90–1349/77) and by Jacopo Alighieri (Fig. 8).

The *Commedia*, of course, generated a literary as well as a critical reaction. The most important direct imitations, despite their artistic flaws, are Boccaccio's *Amorosa visione* ('Amorous Vision'; 1342–43; second redaction *c.*1355-60) and Petrarch's *Triumphi* ('Triumphs'; 1340–74). Both rely heavily on the *Commedia*'s metre, language, structure and motifs to present their visionary subject-matter. Although the *Commedia* inspired few outright imitators, its influence on the formal choices and the artistic purview of fourteenth-century

7.
The opening canto of the *Paradiso* accompanied by an Italian translation of Benvenuto da Imola's commentary to the *Paradiso* (Venetian, first half of 15th century). Oxford, Bodleian Library, MS. Canon. Ital. 105, fol. 2r.

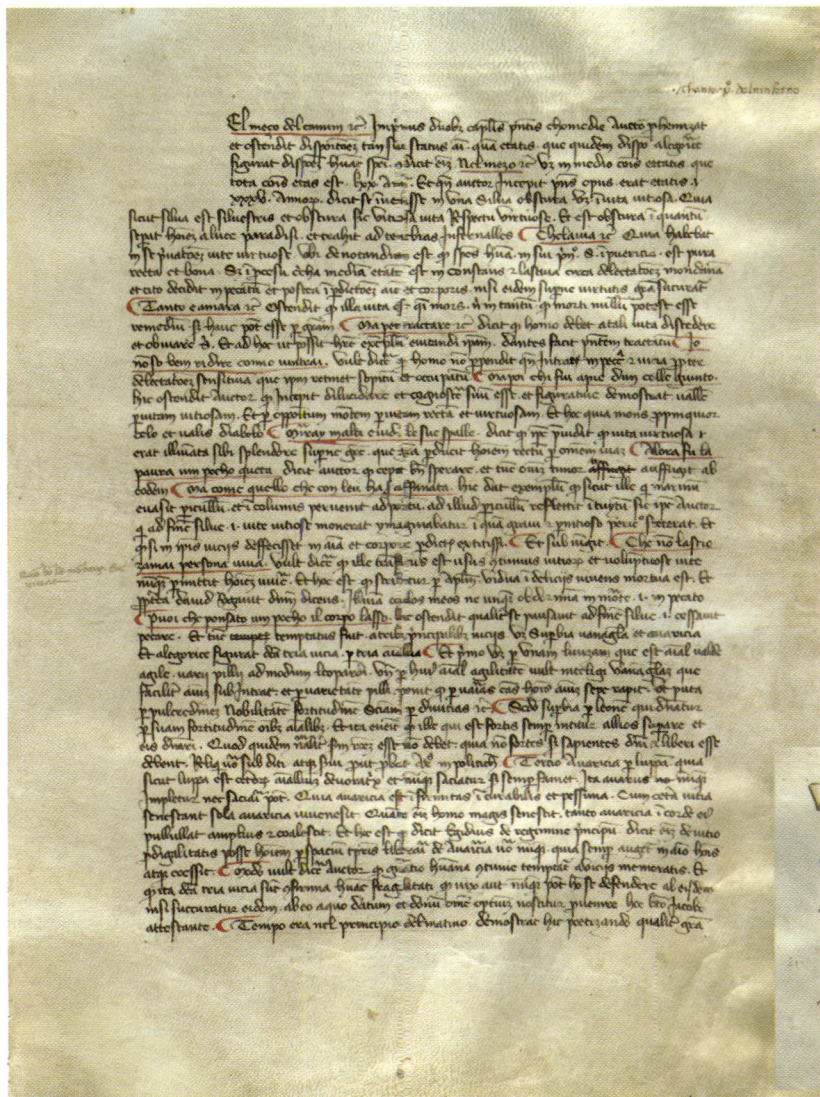

8.
The beginning of a Latin translation of Jacopo della Lana's commentary to the *Commedia*, and (below) the end of Bosone da Gubbio's allegorical poetic introduction (14th and 15th centuries). Oxford, Bodleian Library, MS. Canon. Misc. 449, fols. 5v–6r.

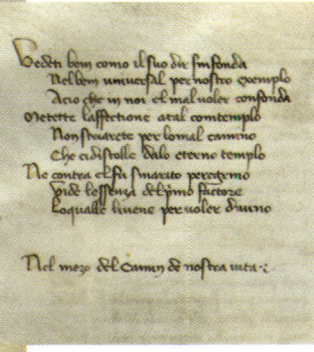

writers was enormous, from translations to chronicles, and from epic to erotic poetry. It exerted a fundamental shaping force on the structure and style of Boccacio's *Decameron* (1349–51); even deeper was its imprint on Petrarch's lyric language in his collection of love poems, known as the *Canzoniere* ('Songbook') or the *Rerum vulgarium fragmenta* ('Fragments of Vernacular Things', 1336–74). Dante's influence also spread to the visual arts, from painting to portraiture and from sculpture to manuscript illustration. Nor were he and his poetry simply a storehouse of subjects fit for artistic treatment. The inscriptions written in *terza rima*, the interlaced rhyme scheme that Dante invented for the *Commedia*, which appear in Simone Martini's fresco of the *Maestà* ('Majesty', 1315–16) in the Palazzo Pubblico in Siena, are based on passages from the *Inferno* and the *Purgatorio* – further evidence of Dante's precocious *auctoritas*.

Despite, or perhaps on account of, its popularity, the *Commedia* engendered both negative and positive reactions among intellectuals. Criticism from both secular and religious circles was directed at its language (vernacular instead of Latin); its failure to observe the conventions of comedy (hence the inappropriateness of its title; the epithet 'divine' was only added in 1555) (Fig. 9); its philosophical ambitions; its theological orthodoxy; its political sympathies; and its doctrinal leanings. Indeed, recent scholarship has begun to demonstrate that all the works Dante wrote after he had begun the *Commedia*, namely the *Monarchia* ('On Monarchy', 1317–18), the *Eclogues* (1319–21) – his response to Giovanni del Virgilio's criticisms – and the *Questio de aqua et terra* ('Question Regarding Water and Earth', 1320), offer rebuttals to such attacks. The poet himself thus provides yet more proof of the speed and seriousness with which his poem was greeted. Many of the commentaries, too, by defending the *Commedia*'s orthodoxy, style, and erudition, appear bent on countering efforts to discredit both the poem and its author. What unites all the extant commentaries is their overt desire to celebrate and monumentalize Dante and the *Commedia*. They constitute, as I suggested earlier, the most sophisticated, overt expression of that fascination with the poem which swept through fourteenth-century Italy – a fascination which today helps us to appreciate and set in context the commentators and their works. For too long, Dante scholars have considered the commentaries simply and anachronistically as mere appendages to the *Commedia*, useful primarily for seeing how early critics unravelled the poem's many *cruces*, rather than as texts in their own right.

The commentaries are products of their environment in other ways. As has already been noted, Dante was intent on vindicating himself and his great poem. This attitude stemmed from his clear awareness of the significance of the critical discourses associated with literary texts. Before he wrote the *Commedia*, in order to highlight the importance of his lyric poetry and of his poetic status, Dante composed the *Vita nova* and the *Convivio*, both of which provide detailed prose self-commentaries on his verse and are closely modelled on the structural conventions of literary manuscripts that combined

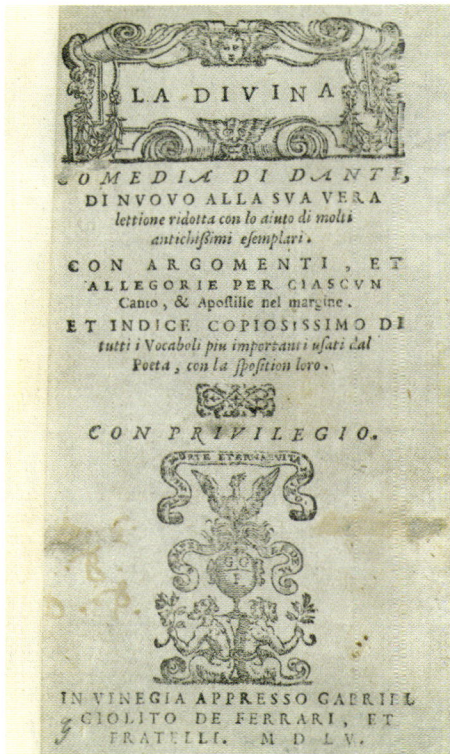

9.
Frontispiece to the 1555 edition of the *Commedia* printed in Venice by Gabriele Giolito that first added the epithet 'Divina' to the poem's title. Oxford, Bodleian Library, Toynbee 894.

a poetic text and its commentary. In order to establish the canonical standing of his *rime*, Dante imitated a textual and critical form which for centuries had normally been restricted to the works of the great Latin poets. In the *Convivio*, he drew additionally on the interpretive conventions of Scriptural, philosophical, and theological commentary.

The commentators of the *Commedia* follow in Dante's wake, not least because in the poem, although he did not establish any explicit links with the normal conventions of exegesis as he had done in the *Vita nova* and the *Convivio*, he did fashion a complex system of self-reflective critical allusion that is based on a judicious use of technical critical vocabulary and on the narrative action and its formal representation. Dante's aim was to explain and justify the *Commedia*'s experimentation and to establish himself as an *auctor*. That he was successful in this ambition is demonstrated by the fact that almost immediately commentaries began to be written on the poem which carefully imitated the conventions of the exegetical tradition to the classical *auctores*. The commentators recognized and confirmed Dante's 'authoritativeness'. For the first time in centuries, a new *auctor* had been canonized; indeed Benvenuto da Imola (1320/30 – 1387/88), the most incisive and original of the *Commedia*'s fourteenth-century exegetes, unambiguously declared that Dante was the greatest of all writers: 'No other poet knew how to praise and condemn as excellently and effectively as Dante, the most perfect poet'. In the late Middle

Ages, *laudare et vituperare* were used as an overarching formula to describe the ambit of literature as a whole, and Benvenuto wrote a monumental commentary to the *Commedia* (1375-83), based on his public lectures, to demonstrate that his critical assessment of Dante's achievement was sound.[8]

To date, Dante scholarship has not found it easy to trace the history of the fourteenth-century commentators precisely. There are several major reasons for this. The nineteenth-century editions of many of the commentaries are defective; it has proved difficult to date a large number of the commentaries accurately (the most commonly accepted dates are given here); several commentaries exist in different versions; and it was not uncommon for commentators and copyists to confuse and contaminate different sets of glosses. All these factors make it hazardous to try to work out the relationship between different commentaries. The problem is especially acute regarding the so-called *Epistle to Can Grande*, named after its supposed addressee, who was Lord of Verona between 1311 and 1329. The letter examines the *Commedia* in general by assessing its allegorical structure and by considering it under the six headings typical of one of the standard models of the *accessus* – the prologue with which a commentary to an *auctor* traditionally opened ('the subject, the author, the form, the aim, the book's title, and the branch of philosophy to which it belongs')[9] – before offering a detailed literal reading of the opening twelve lines of the *Paradiso*.

Scholars continue to disagree whether the *Epistle* was penned by Dante himself. Those supporting Dante's authorship claim that it is not only the key commentary to the *Commedia*, but also the text that fundamentally influences nearly all the subsequent commentaries, since these would appear to follow several of its interpretive schemes. However, the philological evidence in favour of Dante is far from compelling; and the letter's links to the other commentaries are in fact extremely few and involve matters, such as the wording of the *accessus* headings and of the poem's ethical definition, which were commonplaces. In any case, it is not at all clear from these verbal repetitions whether the commentators depend on the *Epistle* or vice versa. The *Epistle* was only mentioned twice during the Trecento: in the autograph glosses to the *Commedia* written in the early 1340s by the Florentine notary Andrea Lancia (*c.*1297–1357),[10] and in the preface of the last of the fourteenth-century commentaries (1391–1405), by Filippo Villani (*c.*1325–1405).[11] This has led some scholars to hypothesize that it is a compilation of several earlier texts.

The possibility that the letter is a forgery would also seem to be supported by its conservative exegesis. It fails to assert the *Commedia*'s radical novelty – the issue at the heart of Dante's indisputably genuine self-commentary – and treats it instead as an ordinary work of fiction with an ethically useful message. This would suggest that the *Epistle* was composed by a traditionalist intellectual troubled both by Dante's literary ambitions and by his claims that his poem was divinely inspired, and hence true. This was a major source of disquiet even among the poet's admirers, including Pietro Alighieri (before 1300–1364), Dante's other commentator son, who, while highlighting his father's erudition, insisted that the *Commedia* was a fiction.

All the commentaries mix apologetics, explanation, and praise. Yet it is not difficult to discriminate between the aims, and thus the intellectual and cultural ambitions and profiles, of the different commentators. Some prefer to focus on explicating the *Commedia's* allegory, while others concentrate on clarifying its literal meaning, on analyzing its literary qualities, and on providing information about Dante's career and intellectual and political sympathies. Still other writers pragmatically integrate literal and allegorical exposition, as in the first commentary to the entire poem (1324–28), written in Italian by Jacopo della Lana (end of thirteenth–first half of fourteenth century). Jacopo's work, which became very popular and was incorporated into early printed editions of the *Commedia*, marked a growing recognition of Dante's importance within Florence, and can be seen as part of the attempt by Florentine intellectuals to reclaim the exiled poet for his native city (Fig. 10). Graziolo Bambaglioli (*c.*1290–1343) wrote a commentary in 1324 to counter anti-Dante sentiment in Bologna, while the author of the *Ottimo commento* (1334) – termed 'best' in 1612 by linguistic purists impressed by the authenticity of its Florentine vernacular – attempted to synthesize contemporary exegesis of the *Commedia*. Commentaries were even written for personal gain, as in the case of the heavily plagiarizing commentary to the *Inferno* (1369–73) written by Guglielmo Maramauro (1317–after 1379) to curry favour with his political masters, as he successfully manoeuvred to be appointed to an academic post in Naples.

The variety of commentaries and the assortment of uses to which they were put mirror the complexity and vibrancy of Dante's fourteenth-century reception. The poet and his remarkable poem affected every area of cultural life in Trecento Italy. There was no major literary question in which Dante's authority was not invoked: for example, the relationship between Latin and the vernacular, the function of poets and poetry, or the doctrinal character of literature. It is therefore not surprising that the reactions to Dante of the century's two other 'Crowns', Petrarch and Boccaccio, were fundamentally shaped by the poet's general reception. Although Petrarch liked to present himself as largely untouched by Dante and hardly ever mentioned him in his writings, in reality both his Latin and vernacular works reveal a significant formal and ideological dependence on the works of his illustrious forerunner. Petrarch was profoundly troubled by the sway which Dante exerted over Trecento intellectual and artistic life, not least because it placed a heavy obstacle in the way of his own efforts to be treated as an *auctoritas*. In the few instances that Petrarch actually did refer to his rival, he drew on the criticisms that others had expressed and insinuated that Dante's reputation was largely unjustified.

Petrarch's jaundiced view of Dante had a major bearing on his friendship with Boccaccio, who – although he too had some reservations about the nature

10.

The text of the *Commedia*
(*Purgatorio* XI) incorporated
into Jacopo della
Lana's commentary and
distinguished by the use
of rubrication (Emilian,
middle of 15th century).
Oxford, Bodleian Library,
MS. Canon. Ital. 113, fol.
21v.

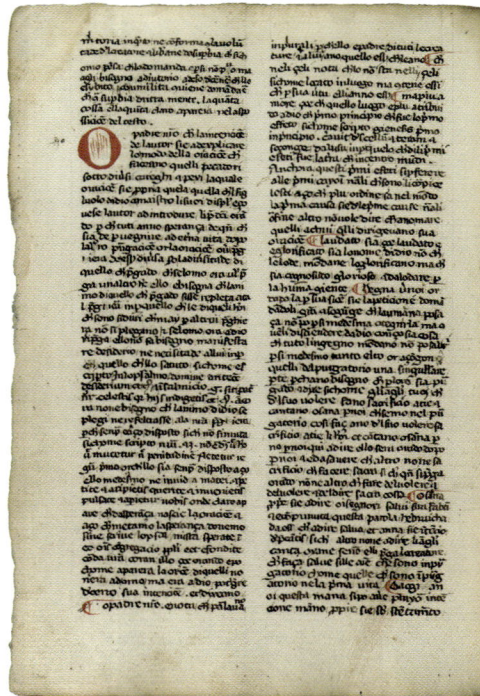

and implications of Dante's authority – did more than anyone else in Trecento
Italy to commemorate and canonize the older poet. Boccaccio openly borrowed
from Dante in his own works; he copied and collated Dante's writings; he wrote
a life of his hero which closely follows the conventions of the lives of Virgil;
he composed encomiastic verse in his honour; and in 1373 he began to write
a major commentary on the *Commedia* which, at his death in 1375, had reached
the opening lines of *Inferno* XVII. For all his efforts to persuade Petrarch that
his negative view of Dante was unjustified, Boccaccio appears to have had no
success in influencing his friend. If anything, over the years Petrarch managed
somewhat to attenuate Boccaccio's enthusiasm, a shift which resembled the
overall drift of Dante's reception in the final decades of the Trecento.

As the century drew to a close, although Latin culture was well on the way
to reasserting itself,[12] its supremacy would be relatively short-lived. Thanks in
no small part to Dante, the progress and establishment of vernacular culture
could be delayed but not halted. Modern literature had arrived; and with
it, in the shape of the commentaries to the *Commedia*, the modern study of
literature also appeared. Dante transformed Western literature; but it was the
poet's first readers, drawing on his bold example, who fundamentally affected
our reading practices and our sense of the literary. For this reason alone,
Dante's fourteenth-century reception deserves to be much better known than
it generally is.

CHAPTER 2

Petrarch: between two ages, between two languages

Martin McLaughlin

Among the many differences between Dante and Petrarch (1304–74), one of the most notable is that while we possess no autograph manuscript by the author of the *Commedia*, we have many of Petrarch's autograph manuscripts of his own works in both Latin and Italian, as well as a large number of what constituted his library, often with revealing annotations by the great humanist scholar.[13] Oxford is fortunate in possessing two important works from Petrarch's library, one classical, one Christian, each of which contains interesting autograph annotations: Suetonius's *Lives of the Caesars*, one of the most copiously annotated manuscripts of Petrarch's entire library (Fig. 13), and the *Epistles* of St Ambrose (Fig. 12).[14] Through these precious documents we see how a great Italian writer transmuted his reading into his writings, and how what Petrarch read determined the main themes of his works and his outlook on life, literature, and history. Although posterity has recognized that both Dante and Petrarch were keen to enrich the new Italian language with a literature that tried to encompass both the classical and Christian heritages, we will now chart the way Petrarch tried to distance himself from Dante – a distance that at first seems enormous in terms of his attitude to the Italian language and his interests in history and time.

The previous chapter showed how Dante inaugurated a cultural revolution by deciding to write an epic work, the *Commedia*, not in Latin, but in the relatively new Italian vernacular. What happened next was to make the history of Italian literature unique in Europe. Two writers of the following generation, Petrarch and Boccaccio (1313–75), would each write a masterpiece in the vernacular – Petrarch his *Canzoniere* (literally 'Songbook') or *Rerum vulgarium fragmenta* ('Fragments of Vernacular Things', begun *c.* 1336), and Boccaccio his *Decameron* (1349–51). Yet despite this trio of great works written in the new language by the mid-fourteenth century, there would be no more culturally significant works written in Italian until the 1470s. The main cause of this hiatus of a century and a quarter was Petrarch

11.
Petrarch's Suetonius (*c.* 1350).
His marginal notes are
mostly cross-references to
other classical sources, but
the first annotation on the
Life of Augustus (bottom
left) notes that Augustus's
family was 'not aristocratic
but ancient', a point
Petrarch will recycle about
his own family in his Letter
to Posterity. Oxford, Exeter
College, MS.186, fol. 10r.

himself: his views on the superiority of Latin over the vernacular, coupled
with the extraordinary influence he enjoyed during and immediately after
his own lifetime, encouraged his successors to write almost exclusively in the
language of learning, Latin.

Francesco Petrarca, known in the English-speaking world as Petrarch,
was born in Arezzo and spent most of his early life in Avignon, where his
father – a Florentine lawyer exiled along with Dante in 1302 – had found
work with the papal Curia. After studying law in Bologna (1320–26), the
young Petrarch returned to Provence, where he lived until the 1350s, mostly
in his country retreat in Vaucluse. Despite his legal studies, his real passion
was the study of ancient (mostly Latin) literature, history, and philosophy.
He travelled on several occasions to Italy, where he was inspired particularly
by the antiquities of Rome. On one of these visits, in 1341, he was crowned
with a laurel wreath on the Roman Capitol, in a ceremony that he had
largely orchestrated himself, but which was meant to signal the revival of
one of the most important ceremonies of the ancient world, the crowning
of a contemporary poet. Petrarch claimed to be the first poet to be thus
honoured since the time of Statius, 1,200 years previously. After 1353 he
settled finally in Italy, living first in Milan, then in Venice, and finally in

the little village of Arquà just outside Padua. At his death he was the most
famous and influential intellectual of his time.[15]

Petrarch's fame and his importance for European culture rest on two
factors: first his vernacular verse, which was to become the major model
for European love poetry in the Renaissance and beyond; and secondly his
humanism, his rediscovery of the texts and values of classical antiquity.
This would initiate an intellectual fashion that would captivate thinkers,
writers, and artists over the next two centuries — indeed humanism would
become almost synonymous with the Renaissance. Petrarch's Italian poetry
consists of two works. The collection of 366 vernacular love poems,
commonly known as the *Canzoniere*, was composed over many decades from
1336 until his death. The *Trionfi* ('Triumphs'), a series of visionary poems,
also had a lengthy gestation (*c.* 1340–74); they were clearly intended to be a
more classicizing version of Dante's great vision poem, the *Commedia*. Both
collections deal with his love for Laura, a woman whom he first saw, he
tells us, on 6 April 1327 in the church of St Clare in Avignon, and who died
exactly 21 years later (as he states in a note on his precious manuscript of
Virgil), on 6 April 1348, a victim of the Black Death that ravaged Europe
that year.[16]

The main theme of the *Canzoniere* is Petrarch's love for Laura, both
during her life and after her death, as well as the ethical conflict that this
love induced in the poet, who constantly aspired to lead a moral existence
untouched by earthly desire. He claims that the day he first saw Laura
was Good Friday, when his thoughts should have been on higher things;
that particular day thus became emblematic of this moral conflict. The
associations of his beloved's name with the laurel (Italian *lauro*) allowed him
to introduce an allegorical dimension into the poetry, so that his love for
Laura could also symbolize his love of poetry itself. The other haunting
motif of the collection is the passing of time, recorded in a number of
'anniversary' poems, all purportedly written on 6 April in various years.[17] As
we shall see, Petrarch was obsessed with time, both on a macro-level — in
terms of periods of history — and on the micro-level of his own quotidian
existence.

The humanist writings, in Latin prose and verse, rarely mention Laura.
Instead, one of the main motivations behind these works was an attempt
to revive major literary genres of the past, many of which had not been
used since antiquity: in poetry, the epic, the pastoral, and verse epistles;
and in prose, historical biographies of famous men, collections of letters,
dialogues, and moral treatises.[18]

Renaissance humanism, like so many things, is said to have begun
with Petrarch, but in what did this movement consist? It had four main
components. The first was the pursuit of original texts. Petrarch was highly
sensitive to the loss of classical texts, and by 1330 had put together the most

complete version of Livy's *History of Rome* since antiquity.[19] He also made
two crucial manuscript discoveries: first, in 1333, he found Cicero's speech *For
Archias* in Liège; realizing that this oration had not been known for centuries,
he instantly transcribed it and circulated it amongst his friends. The
speech was not Cicero's most famous oration, but it was deeply significant
for Petrarch because in its opening paragraph Cicero, defending the poet
Archias, uses the phrase 'studia humanitatis' to refer to the linked group
of subjects that make men 'humane'. This Latin phrase is the origin of the
words 'humanism' and the 'humanities'. For Petrarch and his followers the
phrase denoted the humanist curriculum, which consisted of five subjects:
grammar, rhetoric, history, poetry, moral philosophy. The second major
textual find was his discovery in 1345, in the chapter library in Verona, of
Cicero's *Letters to Atticus*, another text that had disappeared from circulation
since antiquity. From these letters Petrarch learned much about the reality
of politics in ancient Rome, but more importantly the discovery encouraged
Petrarch (and later writers) to collect his own correspondence for later
publication: the *Familiares* or letters to friends (1350–66), and the *Seniles* or
letters written in old age (1361–74), the last of which, a 'Letter to Posterity',
was one of the earliest examples of medieval autobiography.

The second key element in humanism was the emergence of an accurate
historical sense. We have seen that Petrarch was obsessed with the passing
of time; and that he was also a practising historian, writing a series of
biographies of classical and biblical heroes, *De viris illustribus* ('On Illustrious
Men', 1341–43), and a collection of exemplary deeds, *Rerum memorandarum
libri* ('On Memorable Things', 1343–45). However, the most illuminating
text here is in one of his letters, *Familiares* 6.2, written in 1341, in which for
the first time the sweep of history from antiquity to his own day is broken
into two major periods; this division has remained dominant in Western
thought to this day. Petrarch reminisces with his correspondent about their
love of walking amid the ruins of Rome, and then adds: 'We appeared to
be divided: you seemed better informed in modern, I in ancient history – by
"ancient" I mean everything that preceded the celebration and veneration
of Christ's name by the Roman Emperors; by "modern" everything from
then to our own times.'[20] Petrarch sees ancient history as ending with the
conversion of Constantine (in 312 AD), and a 'modern' phase covering
the 1,000 years from then until Petrarch's own age. Another of Petrarch's
key historical statements that must be set alongside this is a remark made
in 'On Memorable Things' (1.19), where he laments the loss of so many
ancient texts. He observes that there is no such sense of loss in either his
classical predecessors (since they actually possessed these works), or in the
generations to come, since their ignorance will make them unaware of their
loss: 'Thus I, who do have reason to grieve for this loss, and do not have the
consolation of ignorance, feel as if I am standing on the border between

two peoples, looking both backwards and forwards at the same time.'[21]

This is an extraordinarily perceptive self-assessment of where Petrarch stands in cultural history: he is very much on the threshold between two epochs, at the end of the Middle Ages and the beginning of the Renaissance. Even these last two terms owe their origin in some sense to Petrarch. For instance, at the end of his Latin epic *Africa* (9.453–7, *c.* 1338-53), addressing his own poem, he feels that a new age of cultural rebirth will soon dawn: 'But perhaps better centuries await you: this sleep of forgetfulness will not last for all time. Our descendants will maybe dispel the darkness and return to the pure light of antiquity.'[22] If we place the earlier periodization alongside these statements, it is clear that Petrarch regards the age from the end of antiquity to his own time as an intervening period that will give way to a better age, of return to or rebirth of the classical past. This intervening time would eventually be called the Middle Ages, or even the Dark Ages, again borrowing a metaphor of light and darkness used by Petrarch.[23]

The third major component that defined humanism was the emergence of a critical sense regarding the past. As a historian Petrarch was often faced with the problem of conflicting sources. At the start of his collection of biographies, he says that when historical sources contradict each other the historian must follow 'only those whose realistic account or greater authority has been such that we are compelled to believe them' ('On Illustrious Men', Proemio).[24] Chapter 1 of the present book noted the importance of the question of authority in the Middle Ages. Low levels of literacy conferred enormous *auctoritas* on any written text, and the link between 'author' and 'authority' was very close; as a result there were a number of forgeries in this period. The most famous of these was the Donation of Constantine, a document that purported to have been written by the emperor when he was about to leave for the East, conferring all temporal power on the papacy and the Church. It was regarded as authentic by Dante and others until the fifteenth century, when a famous humanist successor to Petrarch, Lorenzo Valla (1407–57), highlighted the Donation's unclassical Latin. He proved that instead of being written in the early fourth century, it had been composed in the ninth century at the earliest, probably by someone in the papal Curia.

Petrarch had already done something similar in 1361, when he demonstrated in a letter to the Holy Emperor Charles IV (*Seniles* 16.5) that a Latin document, supposedly signed by Julius Caesar and purporting to exempt the Austrians from paying taxes to the emperor, was a fraud. Petrarch used the tools of humanism, especially recourse to the original text, to show the elements in the document that could never have been written by Julius Caesar. From Caesar's own letters (in Cicero's *Letters to Atticus*) Petrarch knew that he would never have used the 'royal' we (*nos* instead of *ego*), never have called himself anachronistically 'Augustus', and never have ended the document 'Given in Rome on Friday in the first year of our reign'. Caesar, who had reformed the calendar, would certainly have specified the day and month he wrote the document, and would never have used the most offensive word in republican Rome, *regnum* (he would have been happy to be called dictator, but never king). This kind of historical precision is also evident in Petrarch's own copies of his favourite classical authors: in the Oxford Suetonius and Ambrose manuscripts, as in many others, we see his marginal notes setting up a series of cross-references which allowed him to detect contradictions, and to maintain this critical spirit even when reading the most revered texts (Fig. 12).

The final, and perhaps most significant element in humanism for our purposes, was its rejection of the vernacular in favour of Latin. From his prolific output it is clear that Petrarch was interested in writing in both languages. However, the number and bulk of his Latin works far outstrip those of his vernacular compositions, and his official statements on the question of which language to write in suggest contempt for the *volgare*. Since he held ordinary people (Latin *vulgus*) in disdain, he also affected contempt for the vulgar language, claiming that serious literature should only be written for the learned elite that understood Latin. His repeated public proclamations of the superiority of Latin over Italian had a powerful influence on all his disciples, including Boccaccio, who in old age repented of having written the *Decameron* in his native tongue. The result would be that Italian literature, shortly after producing three early masterworks, would be hijacked by Latin: for a century and more after Petrarch's death no Italian writer would write a serious work in the vernacular. Instead intellectuals channelled all their creative energy into Latin, and in due course they were able to write an almost perfect copy of the language of Cicero or Virgil. Only in the last quarter of the fifteenth century, in the age of Lorenzo de' Medici, once they were able to produce perfect Latin, would Italian writers turn once more to using the vernacular for works of high literature.

The crucial document in this linguistic controversy was the letter Petrarch wrote to Boccaccio about Dante in 1359 (*Familiares* 21.15). This brings all three 'Crowns' together, in an important reconfiguration that gives Dante only limited priority. Boccaccio had sent Petrarch a copy of the *Commedia* and in a covering letter had expressed amazement that the great scholar did not possess his own copy of the vernacular masterpiece. The main aim of Petrarch's reply was to refute the widespread rumour, mentioned by Boccaccio, that he (Petrarch) was jealous of Dante. He claims that he did not possess a copy of Dante's work for fear of being unwittingly influenced by him, and in any case he has abandoned works in the vernacular, primarily because of the way the public mangled the poems, including Dante's. As for his supposed envy of his predecessor, he asks how

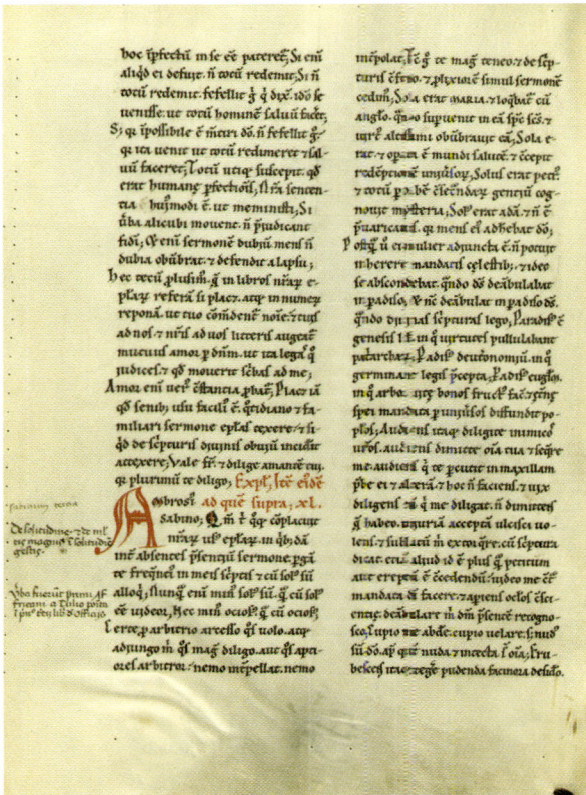

12.
Petrarch's copy of the
Letters of St Ambrose (12th
century). The first note says
'On solitude and the great
things that can be achieved
in it'; the second note shows
Petrarch detecting that
Ambrose is quoting Cicero
here. Oxford, Bodleian
Library, MS. Canon. Pat.
Lat. 210, fol. 23v.

this could be possible, since Dante had dedicated his whole life to writing in
the vernacular, whereas Petrarch only spent a few 'adolescent' years in such
'games'. 'Unless you think,' he adds, 'that I envy him the raucous applause
of the dyers, innkeepers, woolworkers and the rest of the vulgar crowd,
whose praise amounts to a criticism. On the contrary, I congratulate myself
on not enjoying their rowdy applause as by so doing I am in the company of
Homer and Virgil.'[25]

In this meticulously constructed letter, Petrarch is quite happy to award
the 'palm of vernacular eloquence' to Dante, but he distances himself from
the vernacular public and aligns himself with the great poets of antiquity.
The one explicit criticism he makes of his predecessor is that Dante was
better at writing in Italian than in Latin prose or poetry; Petrarch is here
thinking of the medieval tenor of Dante's Latin, whereas the humanist had
learned to cultivate a more classical style in the learned language. This 1359
letter was the first document to fault Dante's Latin, and Petrarch's critique
would be enormously influential, finding echoes throughout the next century
in the writings of his humanist followers, and contributing to the erosion
of Dante's preeminence that took place in the Renaissance.[26] Where Dante
had felt a continuity with the classical world, had elected Virgil as his
guide through the underworld, and had been greeted in Limbo as the sixth

member of an elite group of classical poets, Petrarch was instead sensitive
to the discontinuity, the fragmentary nature of the classical legacy, the
hiatus between his own age and antiquity. He thus appears to drive a wedge
between the two cultures, classical and vernacular, between those who read
Homer and Virgil on the one hand, and on the other, those ('innkeepers and
woolworkers') who read the vernacular.

Nevertheless, these official pronouncements must be treated with
great caution, because we know that despite his express contempt for the
vernacular, Petrarch's autograph manuscripts prove that he continued writing
and rewriting his Italian poems until the year of his death. A fascinating
draft manuscript of his vernacular poems is dotted with precise dates of
composition and interesting stylistic notes in Latin.[27] These show that there
was an intense period late in his life (1366–69) of working on his Italian love
poems as though Laura were still alive; indeed, the composition of his last
vernacular work, *Triumphus eternitatis* ('The Triumph of Eternity'), is dated
'1374, Sunday, before dinner, 15 January. The last canto'.[28] As Petrarch was
then in his seventieth year, this was clearly not a youthful composition, nor a
'game', and hardly displays the attitude of someone who genuinely despises
works in his native language.

It is worth homing in on one of these marginal notes, since it sheds
considerable light on Petrarch's obsession with time. Just above the sonnet
'Voglia mi sprona' ('Desire spurs me on') (*RVF* 211), he writes a note in Latin:
'Amazing: this is a poem which I had left unfinished and forgotten about
many years ago, but I happened by chance to reread it, and I finished it and
immediately transcribed it into its proper place, Friday 22 June 1369, 11 pm.
Shortly afterwards, on 27 June, in the evening, I changed the ending and from
now on the conclusion will be different.'[29] The sonnet's first ending was:

> I entered the labyrinth, and can see no way out,
> At the first hour, on the sixth day of April:
> Alas, I took both the hook and bait of Love!

The new ending eliminates the last line with its hackneyed imagery and
replaces it with a line about the precise year in which he fell in love, thus
making poetry out of time and dates only:

> In thirteen hundred and twenty-seven, precisely
> At the first hour, on the sixth day of April,
> I entered the labyrinth, and can see no way out.
> (*Canzoniere*, 211.11–14)

The details of the time of composition of this and many other poems —
not just the date, but also the day of the week, and the time of day — show

Left column

militū ēēt ad certā stupēdiorū pmiorūꝗ
formula astrix desinitis pꝗradu cuiusꝗ
tpibꝫ militie. ꝗ modis missionū. ne aū
etate aut inopia post missioēs solicitan
ad res nouas possēt. vtꝗ ꝓetio ac sine
difficultate suiptus ad tuendos eos ꝓseꝗ
uendosꝗ suppetit. eranꝫ militarē cū uectī
galibꝫ nouis ꝯstituit. Et ꝗ celerius ac sub
manu annūtiari ꝯgnosciꝗ possz ꝗd in ꝗ
uinta ꝗꝗ ꝗgeretur. Iuuenes ꝑo modicis
inūuallis ꝑ militares uias. dehic uehicu
la disposuit. Cōmodi ꝑo usui ē. ut ex loco
ꝑdem ꝑferūt littas interrogarī ꝗꝗ si ꝗd res
exigant possint. ¶Sigillis ei ꝗdatis ꝗbꝫ in
ꝙ diplomatibꝫ libellisꝗ Zeptis urbat.
Et eplis signādis. inicio spinge usus est.
mox ymagine magni alexandri. nouissi
me sua dioscoris manu sculpta qua sigrā
secuti ꝗꝗ ꝑincipes pseduauerūt. Ad epłā
oēs horariū ꝗꝗ mometa. n̄ dieī m̄o ꝑtꝫ
et noctis qbꝫ datae significarent. addebat.
¶Clementie ꝟDe Clemētia et ciuilitate eiℓde.
ciuilitatisꝗ eius. multa ꝗ magᷓ docu
menta sut. ¶De enumerare quot ꝗquos dū
sani ꝑtiuncia ꝗ incolumitate uoluerit. ꝑin
cipem ꝗ in ciuitate locū tenē passus sit. unī
nuū nouatū. ꝗcassuī pataruū e plebe hōc.
altum pecunia. aliū ceū exilio punire sa
tishabuit. cū ille Agrippe iuuenis noīe asp
ma de eo epłam in uulgꝫ edidisz. hic ꝯtū
melio pleno pelamasz. neqꝫ nouiꝫ sibi. neqꝫ
aiū deceꝑ ꝯdidicit eum. Quādā n̄ agniti
one. cū emilio eliano cordubensi inter ceta
 crimina. ul maxie obiecēt ꝗd male opꝑiū
de cesare soleret. uūsus ad accusatorē. ꝯmo
tꝗ similis uellẽ inꝫhoc ꝗ ꝑbes fiacas scias
etiam. ꝗ me ligua hēre. pła enī de coloquar.
nec quicꝗ ultꝫ. aut statī aut postea iꝗsi
uit. ¶Tibio quoꝗ ꝑentē re. sedulo uiolēti
aꝑse ꝑ plam ꝗquerēti ita rescripsit. Etan
tue m̄ tibi. noli in hac re ūdulgē ꝗ nimi
uū ūdignari quēꝗ ēe ꝗ de me loquatur
male. Satis ē si hoc hēmus ne quis nobis
male facē possit. ¶Dhonoibꝫ ei olatis sīis pūl.
¶Iuge ad has auduentes illa de ornullo. quā puta
bā sūā. ant pꝗ ē iuuta ē curt penłe col. e. i se.

Right column

Templa qꝗ uis sciret possulibꝫ deā sole.
in nulla tn̄ puica n̄ ꝯ suo uincez no
mine recep. Nam in urbe quidem ꝑtinacis
sime abstinuit. hec honēc atꝗ etiam argē
teas statuas olim ē positus ꝯflauit omnes
exquibꝫ aureas cortinas apollini palatino
dedicauit. Dictaturā magᷓ in offerētē in ge
nu mixus. deiecta abhumis toga nudo pecto
re deꝑcaē ē deū appolline. ꝟDe eode ꝗ ciuilibꝫ
¶Domini appllaciōez. gestis eiusdem. ꝟEa
ut maledictū ꝗ obꝑbriū semꝑ exhorruit. Cū
spectare eo litteros pnūtiatū ēēt i mīmo. Q
diū equū ꝗ bonū ꝗ trī usī qn̄ de ipo trī
exultatēs ꝓbassēt. statī manū uinltqꝫ in
decoras adulatoēs repsslit. ꝗ in seꝗti die grā
uissime ꝯripuit. ecco dn̄iꝗꝫ se post hac
appellari. nec alibis quirē aut nepotibꝫ
suis ul sciro ul ioco passim ē. atꝗ huiusmoī
blanditias. ꝗ intue ipos ꝑhibuit. ¶Nō temē
urbe. opꝑtoue ullo egressus. aut quoꝗ igres
sus ē. n̄ uespa aut noctu ne quē officii cā
inquietaret. ¶In ꝯsulatu ꝑdibꝫ seiē. ꝯꝯ
sulatū seꝑ ad opta sella ꝑ publicū inces
sit. ꝟPromiscuis salutatioibꝫ ꝯ miterebaꝫ
et plebem. tanta comitate accuiꝫ osiden
na excipiens ut quēdā ioco compuellit. ꝗ
sic ē libelli porrigē dubitarez. qn̄ elephāto
stipem. ¶Die senatus. nuꝗ pres n̄ in curia
salutauit. ꝗ quirē sedentes ac noiati singu
los. nullo submonete. ꝗ disceceṣ eo modo
sedebꝫ uale dicebat. ¶Officia cū multis
mutuo exiuit. nec prius dies cuiusꝗ solemp
nes frequētare desiit. ꝗ qrito iam ornatu.
Et in turba etiam spōsalioꝝ die uexat.
Gallū trīnū senatorē mīum ē familiarē
iuū captā repete oculis. ꝗ obinediam mori
destinātē. ꝑ sces ꝯsolando reuecauit ad
uitam. ꝟDe patiētia ei iūdictoruz.
¶Ut senatū urbe faciēti dictū ē. n̄ intelli
erat a bilio ꝗdicerē tibi si locū haberē. Iuī
diū ob iū iodicias altercatioes disceptādū
ecuna puus se praphienti. qdā ingessiut.
licet oporte senatoribꝫ de re pūl. loqui. ¶Aū
tistius labeo senatui lectioē. cū trū uiruz

vl̄ nouie h̄

ꝑedictū abbonēs
ab eternis nostre
moribꝫ.
Ide tn̄ fecit Alex
princeps. h̄ ille
uiuū ꝗꝗe fn̄t
nō Alex ille ma
ced. ꝗ st̄ ū dn̄s
m̄ st̄ deū h̄ri a
entiꝗꝫ noluit.

Jaus hic est
in ꝫo statuet

officia.

vl̄ grādioꝝ
cū natū.

Antistius
labeo.

that the other great theme of Petrarch's vernacular poems, the passing of time, was no rhetorical posture but was deeply felt by the poet.

Why was Petrarch so particular about recording these chronological minutiae? A clue is to be found in one of his favourite historical texts, Suetonius's *Lives of the Caesars*. Petrarch possessed at least three copies of Suetonius, but his most heavily annotated copy of the Roman historian has marginal notes dating from 1350 to the end of his life (Oxford, Exeter College, MS 186).[30] In one late annotation he uses the evidence of a Roman coin recently given him to add something not mentioned by Suetonius or any other historian, namely that the emperor Tiberius, after being forced to divorce his first wife Agrippina in order to marry Augustus's daughter Julia, later remarried Agrippina and gave her the title Augusta, after the deaths of Augustus and Julia. Petrarch the antiquarian thus uses numismatic evidence to give a more accurate account of Roman history.

On fol. 16r of the Exeter manuscript we find further evidence of his obsession with precise chronological details: in chapter 50 of the *Life of Augustus*, Suetonius tells how the emperor would add to each letter he wrote 'the exact time of the day or night on which he wrote it' (*Augustus*, 50.1).

14.
Petrarch, *Bucolicum carmen*. Petrarch as red-cloaked scholar holds his book of Latin pastoral poems, a genre he helped revive (manuscript *c*.1400). Oxford, Bodleian Library, MS. Bodl. 580, fol. 1r.

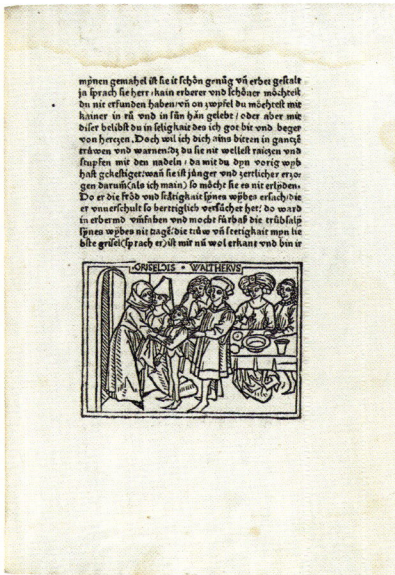

15.
German translation of
Petrarch's version of the
Griselda tale (Ulm, 1473).
Oxford, Bodleian Library,
Douce 204, penultimate
page.

Petrarch marked this passage with his own equivalent of a *nota bene* ('note well') sign, a triangle of three dots with a straight line running vertically down from them (Fig. 13). We know that Petrarch compared many other features of his own life with Suetonius's portrait of the first emperor, including details of his complexion, his eyesight, and even his fear of thunder and lightning, so it is clear that Augustus's meticulous attention to dates lay behind Petrarch's temporal annotations to his Italian poems.[31]

From broad questions of epoch or period, then, and the passing of anniversaries, down to the very hour at which lines of a poem were written, Petrarch was obsessed with the passage of time. It is perhaps no accident that during his lifetime the first public clocks began to appear in Italy. One of Petrarch's friends and correspondents, indeed, was Giovanni Dondi dall'Orologio (1330–88), inventor of a famous astronomical clock, and son of Jacopo Dondi, who had built one of the first public clocks, in Padua.[32] The appearance of such clocks in Italian cities has been cited as an example of the 'secularization' of time, since up until then the time of day had been signalled by church bells tolling for matins, vespers and so on. This secular approach to time has been seen as one of the factors that ushered in the new, lay mentality characteristic of the Italian Renaissance. Petrarch, who looked back to antiquity and forward to posterity, was clearly part of this new sensitivity to time.

To return to Petrarch's views on the superiority of Latin over Italian: his position at first seemed to be vindicated because his name was originally broadcast round Europe by his Latin works. The new learning, epitomized in works such as his *Bucolicum carmen* ('Pastoral Poems', 1346–61), a revival of an ancient genre, proved extremely popular. Manuscripts of such works portrayed him visually very much as the scholar, holding his own book (Fig. 14). It was Petrarch's Latin translation of Boccaccio's *novella* of Griselda (the last tale of the *Decameron*, 10.10), rather than the Italian original, that disseminated the tale north of the Alps in hundreds of manuscripts, and in early printed editions, such as the German translation of Petrarch's version, printed at Ulm in 1473 (Fig. 15). Chaucer, too, borrowed the story (for the Clerk of Oxford's tale) from Petrarch's Latin translation of the Griselda tale rather than from Boccaccio's Italian original.

However, in the course of time even Petrarch's Latin erudition would come to seem outdated, and his vernacular poems would end up having much more influence than his humanist works. As we have seen, behind Petrarch's public contempt for the vernacular lay a serious attempt to endow the new language with some of the grand themes and stylistic qualities that had elevated Latin to its exalted status. While pretending to ignore Dante, and to be reading only classical and Christian texts, the humanist was in reality deeply familiar with the *Commedia* and committed, like Dante, to ennobling the vulgar language, though with different criteria and different outcomes. Petrarch's *Canzoniere* would eclipse Dante's lyric poetry and become a model for all European writers of love lyrics, but the *Trionfi*, despite brief popularity in the Renaissance, would never match the narrative and dramatic sophistication, nor the universal appeal, of Dante's *Commedia*.

The seriousness of Petrarch's vernacular works was recognized by the way they were read. Like Dante's, they too acquired classic status early on, and appeared with the kind of textual apparatus that hitherto had been reserved for ancient texts. The poet's life appeared at the beginning or end of manuscripts or editions of the poems, such as the Latin *Vita*

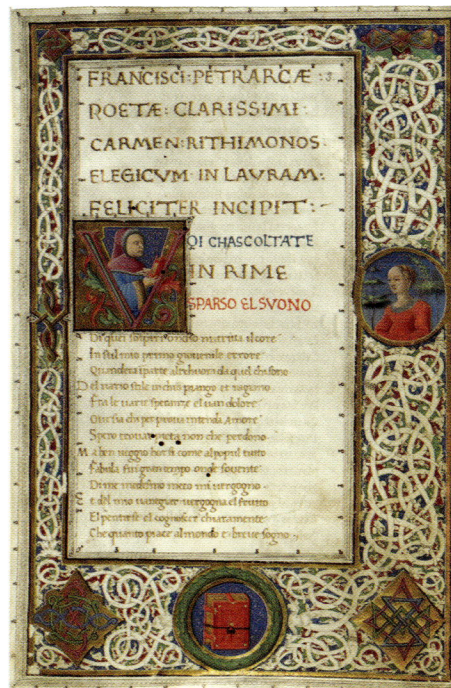

16.
Petrarch, *Canzoniere* and *Trionfi*, and Polenton's Latin *Life of Petrarch*. The cameo on the opening page has Petrarch opposite Laura, who is symbolically between two trees, one of which is a laurel (*c.*1450–75). Oxford, Bodleian Library, MS. Canon. Ital. 70, fol. 3r.

17.
Petrarch, *Trionfi*. A red-robed Petrarch, a blue-robed Laura, and nine philosophers (*c.*146o–80). Oxford, Bodleian Library, MS. Add. A. 15, fol. 1v–2r.

by Sicco Polenton.[33] From 1475 onwards both the *Canzoniere* and the *Trionfi* were accompanied by a weighty commentary, both in manuscript and in early printed editions, that often dwarfed the original text.[34] Although the visual representations of the poet often depicted him with Laura (Fig. 16), in fact Petrarch's lyric poems offered less scope to artists than the vivid narratives of Dante and Boccaccio; nevertheless he could appear with his head crowned with the classical laurel, or in the company of classical philosophers (Fig. 17). In particular the *Trionfi*, with their long lists of ancient heroes, lent themselves to classicizing illustrations (Fig. 18).

The most significant reading of Petrarch's vernacular poetry was the one carried out by the humanist Pietro Bembo (1470–1547) at the beginning of the sixteenth century. He edited for the great Venetian printer Aldus Manutius (1449–1515) the most philologically accurate edition of the *Canzoniere* and *Trionfi* printed up to that point (Venice, 1501); it was printed in the new italic type and in a smaller, octavo format, previously only used for classics such as Horace and Virgil. New technology made the poems accessible to many more readers than manuscript copies could do (Fig. 19).[35] The other influential operation performed by Bembo was to provide, in his authoritative dialogue *Le prose della volgar lingua* ('Prose on the Vernacular Language', 1525), the rules for writing literature in Italian. These amounted basically to the instruction to imitate Petrarch when writing verse, and Boccaccio when writing prose. Bembo considered these two authors the supreme models for vernacular writers because of the mellifluousness and consistency of their language. Dante was excluded as a model on the

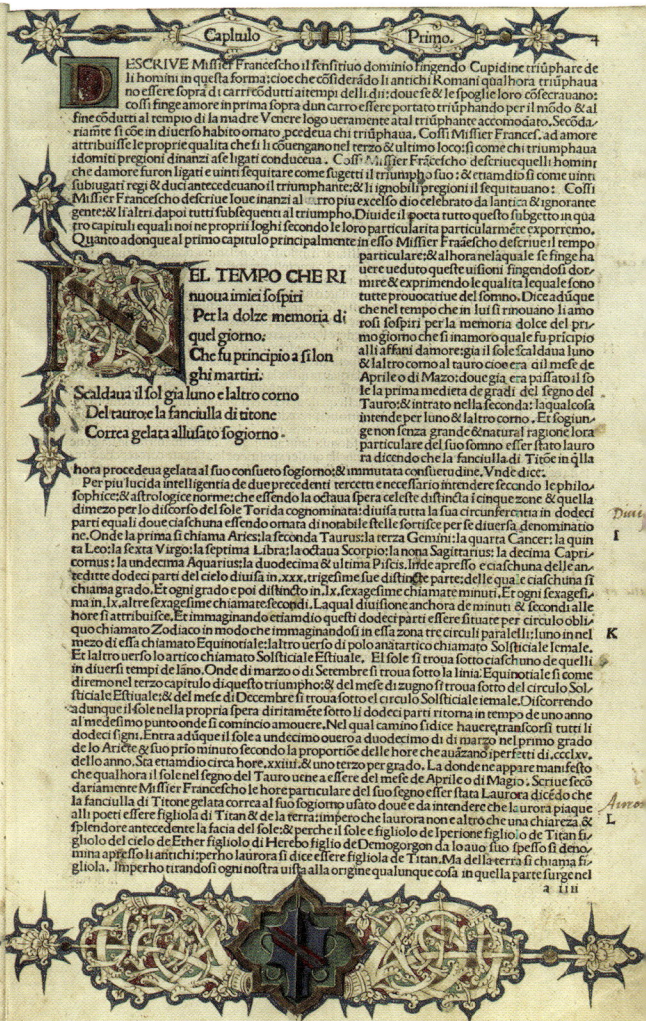

18.
Petrarch, *Trionfi* (Venice, 1488). A highly popular poem in Renaissance court circles, both with readers and with artists. This page shows the *Triumph of Love* and the coat-of-arms of the Albergati family. Oxford, Bodleian Library, Auct. 2Q inf. 1.45, pp. 3–4.

grounds that his language was not always harmonious, and often used either vulgar or excessively elevated words. With Bembo's help the *Canzoniere* and *Trionfi* consolidated the popularity they had already acquired in Italian courtly circles in the fifteenth century (Fig. 20). Bembo's canonization of Petrarch was made easier by printing, which could supply budding poets with indexes and lists of rhyme-words, helping to make the subject matter and language of the *Canzoniere* the basis for all love poetry written in Italy for the next two centuries. Incidentally, the poet's popularity in Protestant Northern Europe was enhanced because the *Canzoniere* included a triptych of sonnets (*RVF* 136–38) denouncing the corruption of the papal court at Avignon. Needless to say, these same poems were highly controversial in Counter-Reformation Italy, and in many copies the sonnets have been scored out (Fig. 21).

Eventually, however, the number of manuscript and printed editions of Petrarch's Italian works far outstripped those written in Latin. Despite all his public pronouncements on the relative merits of the two languages, and their initially persuasive authority, Petrarch the Italian poet was destined in the end to be far more influential than Petrarch the Latin scholar.

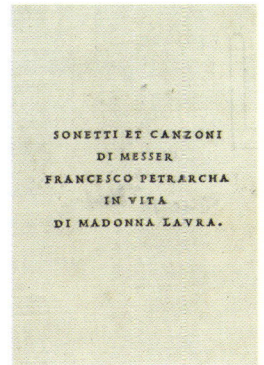

SONETTI ET CANZONI
DI MESSER
FRANCESCO PETRARCHA
IN VITA
DI MADONNA LAVRA.

19.
Petrarch, *Canzoniere* and *Trionfi* (Venice, 1501). Perhaps the most famous edition of Petrarch, edited by the great humanist Pietro Bembo, and based on accurate manuscript evidence. Oxford, Bodleian Library, Auct. 2R inf. 114, title-page.

20.
Petrarch, *Canzoniere*. Petrarch seated at an altar, receiving a laurel crown from Laura, and seven other ladies around. In the lower margin a landscape with a tower in the international Gothic style (*c.* 1420–30). Oxford, Bodleian Library, MS. Canon. Ital. 69, fol. 1r.

21. *overleaf*
Petrarch, *Canzoniere*, with Filelfo's commentary (Venice, 1503), poems 137–38. The most controversial poems were those that condemned the corruption of the papal court at Avignon. Defenders of the papacy tried to censor or expunge these poems from printed editions (but the outraged reader of this copy did not notice that poem 136 was also anti-papal). Oxford, Bodleian Library, Auct. 3Q 4.36, p. 667.

SONETO.C.VIII.

Fiamma dal ciel su le tue treccie pioua
  Maluaggia ch dal fiume & dale ghiāde
  Per laltrui ipouerir sei richa & grāde
Poi che di mal operar tanto ti gioua
Nido di tradimento:in cui si coua
  Quāto mal p lo mōdo hoggi si spāde
  Di uin serua di lecti & de uiuande

In cui luxuria fa lultima proua
Per le camere tue fanciulli & uecchi
Vāno trescādo & belzabub in mezo
Cō mantici:& col foco & cō li spechi
Gia nō fusti nutrita in piume al rezo
Mā nuda al uerno & scalza tra istechi
Hor uiui si cha dio ne uenga il lezo

℃FIAMMA Dal cielo .In q̄sto.cviii.soneto biastema & uitupera una dōna firentina di cui nō si sa certo il nome ne anche di che famiglia si fusse.Dicono alchuni quela eēr chiamata Madōna Contessina.Et che fu del casato ouero famiglia de medici:laq̄l essendo maritata ad uno mercadante Fiorentino che era in Auignone piacq̄ al petrarcha:ilpche la ricerco di battaglia ne a lei dispiacq̄ lesser appellata ma li dimādá.lx.du cati per farsi una cota laquale risposta tanto al petrarcha dispiacq̄ che in uituperio di lei fece subito il p̄se te soneto ilquale perche e per se medesimo chiaro non mi distendero piu oltre.

℃SEGVITA La interptatione di Hyeronimo Squarzafico Alexandrino sopra el resto della p̄sente opera.

℃FIAMMA Dal cielo:in q̄sto.cviii.soneto nō me piaciuto di metere la expōne di.M.F.Philel. pche inue rita il Philelpho i q̄sta cōmentatiōe di q̄sto suo soneto:pche piu auāti nō ha cōmétato secōdo la ueritade nō ha uoluto exporre ma piu tosto p dire male di cosomo de medici delq̄le i q̄llo tēpo era inimico:si chel Petrar:in q̄sto soneto scriue contra la corte di Roma q̄le in q̄lli tp̄i era:& nō cōtra di nissūa dōna d medici laq̄l corte uedea ogni giorno multiplicare i broda & sodomia:& āchora mi pare che seguita piu altri uitii. ℃FIAMma dal cel:questo.S.cō li dui seq̄éti fa.M.F.cōtra la corte romana laq̄l el uedeua ogni zorno mi tiplicare i broda & sodomia & piu altri horribili uitii:Dal fiūe & d la giāde.q nota il poe:el uiuere pouerisimo che za fecero li primi romani che se pasceano de giande & beano aqua.Hor uiui si cha dio ne uenga illezzo idest puzza & fastidio.

SONETO.C.IX.

Laura baylonia ha colmo il sacco
  Dira di dio & di uiti empii & rei
  Tanto che scopia & ha fatto suoi dei
Nō ioue & palla ma uenere & bacco
Aspectādo ragion mi strugo & fiaccō
  Ma pur nouo soldan ueggio per lei
  Loqual sara non gia quando io uorrei

Solo una sede & quella fia i baldacco
Glidoli suoi saranno in terra sparsi
Et le torre superbe al ciel nemiche
Eisuoi torrier di for come dentro arsi
Anime belle & di uirtude amiche
Terrāo il mōdo.& poi uedrē lui farsi
Aureo tutto & pien de lopre antiche

℃LAVRA Babylonia.In q̄sto.cix.soneto il poeta iuehisse cōtra li uitii di Roma si come nel soprascrito soneto & il fece nel tp̄o che fece scōdo che si po cōsiderare q̄lle epistole che sono senza titulo che son tu te cōtra li uitii de la corte Romana q̄le i q̄lli tēpi era i Auignōe:lapella adūc il poeta Babylōia p dinotare magior pléitudie di errori:pche i babylōia pria ogni discordia ardēr si fu trouato:q̄do dice nouo soldā.qui uole si cōe pphetizare che ācora de le abomiatiōe loro li sara tolto l̄ iperio tp̄ale una sede sola si sara i bal dacho:logo scō alcui di Firēze cossi dito altri di Roma che pr̄ mi piace:pche piu tosto i Ro. che i Firen ze q̄ste utilite se doueao far p eēr q̄lla capo di la sua sedia:q̄sto saria p le sue simōie luxuriose & auari tie āie:& q̄sto dice eēr q̄si necessario:& dapoi q̄sto uederēo farsi laureo seculo si cōe fu neli primi tp̄i. ℃LAVRA babilōia ha como il sacho:seguita il poeta la respōsiōe cōtra roma appellādola babylōia a de notar magioi pléitudie de errori:ma pur nuouo soldā:q uol q̄si dire el poeta pphetizādo chel gli sera tol to el staro tp̄ale.Solo una sede ch sia i baldacco:cioe soto el baldachio doue ua soto el papa:& soi torrier di fuor come dentro arsi:arsi fuora q̄to p iustitia si como ardēo de dētro p sodomia & luxuria.Aie belle:uol dir che quasi e necessario chel mōdo s̄ rimoui & torni la eta prima como fu al tp̄o de Cesare Octauiāo so to ilq̄l la uirtu hebe tāta gratia & pricipio.

SONETO.C.X.

Fontana di dolore:albergo dira
Scola derrori & templo de heresia
  Gia Roma:hor Babylonia falsa & ria
  Per cui tanto si piange & si sospira
O fucina dinganni o pregion dira
  Oue el ben more:il male sinutre:& cria
  Di uiui inferno:un grā miracol fia

Si christo teco el fin poi non sadira
Fondata in casta & humil pouertade
Cōtra tui fondatori alzi le corna
Puta ssacciata:& doue hai posto spene
Negli adulteri tuoi:nelle mal nate
Richeze tante hor cōstantin nō torna
Ma tolga il mondo tristo chel sostene

CHAPTER 3

Boccaccio visualized in manuscript and print

Christopher C. Stevens

The early reception of the works of Giovanni Boccaccio (1313–75) can be traced graphically through the surviving manuscripts and fifteenth-century printed editions of his works. Those that are illustrated provide particularly valuable evidence, because as well as containing visualizations of the works which sometimes gloss the texts, they also show great diversity in artistic style. This holds true for Boccaccio's reception within Italy and beyond – most notably in France, but also in England. The series of illuminated manuscripts and incunabula discussed in this chapter, ranging from an Italian *Decameron* to a French *Filostrato*, an English *De casibus virorum illustrium* ('The Fates of Illustrious Men') and a German copy of the first illustrated edition of a work by Boccaccio, witness to the developments in this reception. They show that this reception was almost immediately European, not just Italian, and that Boccaccio's Latin works were valued at least as highly as his vernacular ones. It is also apparent that his works were quickly assimilated into circles well beyond those in which they were first read, and that this had a major impact on the manuscripts and editions that were produced.

Boccaccio 'visualizations' (a term which includes all images of textual relevance but excludes purely decorative initials, marginal sprays, etc.) have been the subject of numerous studies in recent years.[36] In the three decades since the landmark exhibition of Boccaccio manuscripts at Florence's Laurentian Library in 1975, scholarship in this field has blossomed into a veritable industry that ranges from analyses of individual manuscripts or the holdings of particular libraries to a comparative study of paintings, manuscripts, and Pasolini's film version of the *Decameron*.[37] The culmination of the mainstream of scholarship is the three-volume *Boccaccio visualizzato*, edited by Vittore Branca,[38] which examines manuscripts, incunabula, and works of art and gives a unique insight into the visual tradition of the works of a single author.

The number and the variety of visualizations of the works of Boccaccio

22.
Boccaccio, *De mulieribus claris*, Italian translation by Donato degli Albanzani (1418–25). Oxford, Bodleian Library, MS. Canon. Ital. 86, fol. 1r.

are remarkable. When the visual legacy of the *Decameron* is compared with that of the *Canterbury Tales* – a work that invites comparison not least because of Chaucer's debt to Boccaccio – its extent is astonishing. Once investigation is widened to include Boccaccio's numerous other vernacular and Latin works, even the tradition of Dante visualizations (the many fine copies of the *Commedia* notwithstanding) might seem relatively limited.

What emerges most clearly from an overview of Boccaccio visualizations is the breadth of this visual tradition, encompassing everything from relatively humble manuscripts with pen-and-ink sketches or author portraits in historiated initials, to luxurious manuscripts and richly illustrated printed editions. Virtually all of Boccaccio's diverse output, from his early vernacular compositions to his compendious Latin works, found favour with illustrators. The visualizations are eloquent testimony to the wide reception of Boccaccio's writing over an extended period of time, which stretches without interruption from his death in 1375 to the early printed editions of a hundred years later and beyond. This enthusiastic reception is confirmed by the translations, first in manuscript and then in print, that appeared in countries north of the Alps.

Giovanni Boccaccio's own output as a scribe would have guaranteed him some fame in posterity even if he had never written anything original himself. Most famous among the manuscripts that have been identified as by his hand is the autograph copy of the *Decameron* in Berlin,[39] but it is his *Zibaldoni laurenziano* and *magliabechiano* (commonplace books containing classical and contemporary texts, letters, translations, original compositions of his own, etc.) that best show his passion for copying extant works. In common with so many manuscripts of the period they show numerous marginal annotations, including the *manicula*, or quickly sketched pointing hands, that identify important passages of text. It is not unexpected, therefore, to find such annotations in the margins of a late fourteenth-century manuscript of Boccaccio's *De mulieribus claris* ('On Famous Women', 1361–75), a compendium of famous women written in an ornate Latin clearly indebted to the example of Petrarch's *De viris illustribus* ('On Famous Men').[40] These annotations are almost certainly in the hand of Coluccio Salutati (1331–1406), from whose circle the manuscript originates. As well as holding the post of Florentine Chancellor for thirty-one years, Salutati was a bibliophile and important early humanist who played a key role in bringing the Byzantine scholar Manuel Chrysoloras to Florence in 1396. The image of Boccaccio in the historiated initial on the opening page (fol. 1v) is appropriate to the academic circulation of this manuscript; it shows a generic portrait of a robed academic holding an open book and raising his right hand, in a gesture suggesting speaking or teaching. Salutati's scribal interventions are not frequent, but they remind us of Boccaccio's reputation as a scholar whose works were studied in humanistic circles. The addition

Proemio nello libro de M. Giouanni Boccatio de le famose donne.

Uno scritto per lo tempo passato alcuni antichi n breuemente libri di famosi homeni. Et alnostro tempo ha scritto imagiore uolume et cum piu ornato stilo lo chiarissimo poeta francesco petrarcha mio maestro et degnamente accio che lamemoria dequegli iquali lanno meritato peruegna ad quegli che seguiranno cu perpetuale fama essendo egli eccellenti digli altri homeni per chiari fatti gauendo albesogni posto tutto elsuo studio el sangue le richeçe et lanima p questo fine. Ma p certo molto merauiglio che le donne albino aiuto si pocha possança appresso di si fatti homeni delle inspetialita per scriptura non albiano acquistato gratia de alcuna memoria essendo manifesto per legrande histori de alcune anno adoperato certe cose cum grante forteçça et ardire. Et segli homeni se dieno magnificare quanto egli fanno igrandi fatti auenço egli la possança quanto piu se dieno magnificare le donne lequali quasi tutte per natura sono delicate et debili del corpo et anno pigro ingegno se elle pigliano animo uirile et cum nobile ingegno et chiara uirtu ardiscono et adoperano le cose fatigose agli homeni. Et per questo accio che elle non plano soa ragione cum uenuto inanimo redare insieme quelle che me tornauo ad memoria p honore de sua gloria et de quelle aggiungero alcune lequali ardatia o uertu de ingegno o de industria ouero dono de natura o gratia de fortuna o odio a facti notabili et ad queste congiungere alcune poche dellequali bene de alcuni non albiano giudicato degna cosa de farne memoria non demeno sono state cagione de grandi facti. Et non uoglio che paia inconueniente allo lectore sello trouera mesciate cum penolope lucretia et sulpitia castissime donne. Medea et flora lequali ebero grande ingegno bene che lo auessero

23.
Boccaccio, *De casibus virorum illustrium*, French translation by Laurent de Premierfait (1409). Oxford, Bodleian Library, MS. Bodl. 265, fol. 2r.

in a different contemporary hand (fols. 58v–59r) of Petrarch's account of the deeds of Maria da Pozzuoli, from his *Familiares* 5.4, emphasises the links between the two writers among early humanists.

The Bodleian Library, Oxford, holds several earlier vernacular manuscripts of works by Boccaccio, but the first to have visualizations is the *Libro delle donne famose* ('Book of Famous Women'), an Italian translation of *De mulieribus* by Donato degli Albanzani (?1328–1411), transcribed between 1418 and 1425 (MS. Canon. Ital. 86). That this is the earliest visualized manuscript held by the library is partly explained by the comparatively poor visual treatment accorded to Boccaccio's *opere minori*, and to the relatively humble nature of many of the copies. Copies of minor works such as *Corbaccio, Fiammetta, Filocolo, Filostrato, Ninfale fiesolano* ('Nymphs of Fiesole'), and *Trattatello* ('Life of Dante') (most of which are from the fifteenth century), also in the Bodleian, have no visualizations. From illustrated copies elsewhere it is apparent that such works were not often given more than an author portrait, and that many of the more densely illustrated copies date from a later flowering of visualizations in manuscripts of a different style, as will be seen in relation to the *Decameron*.

MS. Canon. Ital. 86 dates back to the earliest redactions of the original, and thus cannot have been begun for Niccolò III d'Este (1384–1441), whose arms appear in the border decoration on the first folio, and to whom the final version was dedicated. It may have been intended for Niccolò's second wife, Parisina Malatesta, whose arms are included along with those of her husband. At the top of the same folio a miniature depicts three enthroned ladies, probably representing women who achieve fame on the field of battle (centre) or in learning (right) and those whose wickedness Boccaccio includes in his work as cautionary tales (left) (Fig. 22). The latter has a certain poignancy, since Parisina herself was executed in 1425 on account of her love affair with Ugo, Niccolò's son by a previous marriage. Overall, the manuscript belongs to a type which has one main illustration, similar to the frontispiece in printed books (often with the inclusion of the owner's arms).[41] The addition of a second illustration (fol. 3r), showing a generic author portrait of a scholar dressed in red robes can be explained by the existence in the text of Boccaccio's Proemio, or prologue, and is repeated in several other copies that include the Proemio. The manuscript testifies to the importance of Boccaccio's Latin works in securing his reputation; but it also points to the spread of their popularity beyond Florence, and beyond narrowly humanistic groups to the Italian court circles in which many of his most famous manuscripts were subsequently produced. The new readership also included an English audience for at least part of *De mulieribus*, as Chaucer had translated and incorporated the story of Zenobia into the Monk's Tale of the *Canterbury Tales*. Anonymous French (1403) and English (1440s?) translations also demonstrated the wide appeal of this catalogue of famous women.

Ci comance le premier prologue du translateur du livre de Jehan Bocace des cas des nobles homes et femmes

Puissant noble et
excellent prince
Jehan filz de Roy
de France Duc de
Berry et dauvern
gne Conte de Poi
tou destampes de
Boulongne et
dauvergne
Laurens de premier fait clerc dvre
mome digne secretaire et sers de bonne
foy toute obedience et subiection deue
comme a mon tresredoubte seigneur et
bienfaiteur et antteable ment receun

le labeur de mon estude et lentiquement
expose la petitesse de mon engin au regart
de la tres ardu besongne de vostre commandement
par moy ia piecza entreprise et nouvellement
finee Combien que par vre espaivan
dement ie aye soubz la confiance de vre
naturele benignte et en espoir de vostre
gracieux aide et confort entrepris le don
tereux et long travail de la translacion
de vostre tresgrant et singulier volume des
cas des nobles hommes et femmes escript
et compile par iehan Boccace de certald
iadis homme monlt excellant et expert
en Anciennes histoires et toutes autres

24.
John Lydgate, *Fall of Princes,*
English adaptation of
Boccaccio, *De casibus virorum
illustrium* (1431–38). Oxford,
Bodleian Library, MS. Bodl.
263, p. 7.

Another early fifteenth-century manuscript (Oxford, Bodleian Library, MS. Bodl. 265) provides evidence both of Boccaccio's growing fame in France, and of just how crucial his Latin works were in this respect. It is a copy of *Des cas des nobles hommes,* Laurent de Premierfait's French translation of Boccaccio's *De casibus virorum illustrium* (1360–75), which was begun just before *De mulieribus* and deals with famous men. The text is Premierfait's second translation and expansion of *De casibus,* written in 1409, five years before he completed his *Decameron* translation (see below). The copy and its miniatures can be closely linked to a different manuscript, produced in northern France at this time, and perhaps to another which was actually given to Jean, Duc de Berry, to whom the translator's prologue is addressed. The miniature at the head of fol. 2r is divided into four scenes round the figures of a pope, a king, the duke (being presented the work by Premierfait, perhaps introduced by Boccaccio), and four artisans, reflecting the divisions of the Prologue. The scratches disfiguring the faces of pope and cardinals suggests that the manuscript came to England before the Reformation (Fig. 23). The other nine smaller miniatures each illustrate the opening story of the nine books into which the text is divided, and distill the major elements of each narrative into clearly recognizable images.

Using visualizations (like initials and rubrics) to mark the sections of a work was common practice. The images might have served as mnemonics for the text they summarize, in the manner of the *Biblia Pauperum* and many works of art, notably fresco cycles. This practice finds its fullest expression in several French manuscripts of *De mulieribus* and *De casibus,* which contain upwards of one hundred miniatures.[42] The less dense illustration of MS. Bodl. 265 means the principal function of the images is decorative, but this does not detract from their capacity to elucidate the text. The French courtly circles into which Boccaccio's works have moved therefore make their own mark on the visual tradition of the work whilst maintaining features of the Italian precursors. In MS. Bodl. 265 the humanistic roots of the text are made clear by a scene at the start of Book VIII (fol. 253r) in which Boccaccio, lying in his bed, is approached by the appropriately wreathed figure of Petrarch. The figures are linked visually, as they are linked in the text, and as they were in the minds of their first readers (as we have seen in Salutati's manuscript of *De mulieribus*).

The middle years of the fifteenth century witnessed a flowering of manuscripts of Boccaccio's works in Italy, France, and elsewhere. They also saw the donation by Duke Humphrey of Gloucester to the library of Oxford University of manuscripts of Boccaccio's four most famous Latin works, which were by this time considered essential works of reference. A key reference work to classical mythology for several centuries, the *Genealogie deorum gentilium* ('Genealogies of the Pagan Gods', 1360–74) was donated in 1439, followed in 1444 by *De casibus* and *De mulieribus,* along with *De montibus*

('Concerning Mountains', *c.* 1355–74), a geographical dictionary for classical
literature. Duke Humphrey's Boccaccian legacy was not entirely lost when
his library was dispersed in the sixteenth century, because a copy of *The
Fall of Princes*, an English translation of *De casibus* made *c.* 1431–38 by John
Lydgate at the request of the royal collector and scholar, remains in Oxford
as MS. Bodl. 263. The compilation of this manuscript is datable to *c.* 1450;
it is perhaps of East Anglian origin, and its ownership can be traced via
inscriptions to Sir John Godsalve of Norwich and the recusant Sir Francis
Engelfield.[43]

　　This English translation of *De casibus* emphasizes the importance of the
French Boccaccio tradition, both because Premierfait's translation served
as the source for Lydgate (who probably never knew the original text), and
because the programme of illustration was intended to be lavish, on a scale
with the programmes of illustration for Boccaccio's work then prevalent
on the continent. A full-page miniature was envisaged for each book,
but only the first miniature was completed (p. 7), showing twelve scenes
drawn from Book I. They include immediately recognizable scenes, such
as the temptation of Adam and Eve and The Flood; others are not readily
identifiable, despite their abundant detail (Fig. 24).

　　While the luxury of the *Fall of Princes* manuscript — at least as it was
originally intended — reflects the prestige associated with such works in the
mid-fifteenth century, a far more modest manuscript, probably produced in
Oxford itself around 1460, emphasizes the importance given to Boccaccio's
Latin reference works within academic circles at this time. Merton College
MS. 299 was bequeathed to the college of which he was a student and
Fellow by Thomas Bloxham in 1473. It contains Bersuire's commentary, John
of Garland's *Integumenta*, and John Seguard's *Argumenta* on Ovid's *Metamorphoses*,
as well as other works by Seguard. The family trees from the *Genealogie deorum*
(fols. 282r–88v) are copied in an unusual layout, very different to that used
by Boccaccio himself in his autograph copy of the text and to those which
appeared in later editions, such as the one printed in Venice in 1494.[44] It is
clear from its contents and style that this manuscript was intended primarily
for study, perhaps even for the use of Bloxham himself.[45]

　　The earliest surviving illustrated copies of the *Decameron*, like Salutati's
manuscript of *De mulieribus* and Bloxham's excerpts from the *Genealogie
deorum*, were made by enthusiasts for Boccaccio's work. They were, however,
enthusiasts of a different kind, whom Branca has characterized as mercantile
'enthusiastic scribes'.[46] By including lively, lightly shaded pen-and-ink
sketches in their copies, Giovanni d'Agnolo Capponi and Lodovico di
Silvestro Ceffini were following the example of the most passionate of all
copyists, Boccaccio himself.[47] Boccaccio was an ardent drafter and emender
of his own works. He also showed some skill as a draughtsman, both in his
tables for the *Genealogie* and in his autograph copy of the *Decameron*, which

A tresexcellent puissant
et noble prince Jehan
fils de Roy de france duc
de berry et dauuergne
conte de poictou de es-
tampes de boulongne et dauuergne selon
Justice seur de ses dignite et puissance mo
armez honeur deseruer historie de voz come
me manifestes et racines sur habundan-
ce de vertus diuines et humaines Et
a voutz comme seigneur et prince obeis-
sance entiere de moy Laurens de premier
fait vostre humble clerc et subgiet ho
lumbure ¶ Apres long pensement
et secret enuers moy ay aduisé hrai-
ement que sire adam et dame eue
premiers parens de tout le humain
lignaige furent en lestat de inno-

rence si comblez et plains de tous
dons et prerogatiues de graces
celestes et humaines que nest come
le droit fils furent Immortelz Jusque
a cellui dampnable monument
ouquel ilz enfraignrent la loy a
eulx donnee depar dieu leur crea-
teur et prince de toutes choses
Lenfermete dun aidement dun bel
touma et peruerti au regard des
hommes tout profit en dommaige
amour en hayne pitie en cruaul-
te Joye en tristesse Seurete en
remeur Or suite en risancon tou
gent ¶ Et oultre plus par les
hommes entre eux mil autres do
maiges demeurent enfermes et
mortelz ignorans rissancon meur

was completed some twenty years after he first wrote the work and was
perhaps destined for Petrarch or Mainardo Cavalcanti, a Florentine protector
and correspondent to whom he dedicated *De casibus* in its Prologue (Berlin,
Staatsbibliothek der Stiftung Preussischer Kulturbesitz, MS. Hamilton 90).
This Berlin manuscript includes twelve portraits of characters from the
tales and one of Neifile, a member of the story-telling *brigata*. Although
artistically undistinguished, their subtle characterization helps bring the
text to life, as do the more decorative, but still quite summarily achieved,
miniatures in the Capponi and Ceffini manuscripts. The *Decameron*
manuscripts from the 1460s in the Bodleian Library are of a very different
kind, more akin to the copies of the Latin works whose popularity had
served to spread Boccaccio's fame beyond his native city and its mercantile
readership to the French and Italian courtly circles in which his works were
by then circulating.

A French manuscript of Premierfait's *Decameron* translation is identifiable
from a 1467 inventory as part of the library of Philip the Good of
Burgundy, although an empty shield on fol. 1r suggests the manuscript may
not have been commissioned by him (Oxford, Bodleian Library, MS. Douce
213). Accordingly, its decoration, albeit restricted to a single miniature, is of
superior quality. Completed at a time when some *Decameron* manuscripts, like
those of the Latin works, included as many as one hundred miniatures, it is
not a truly de luxe exemplar (it is, for example, written on paper). However,
the first recto does include a large miniature within the decorated borders
above the text of Premierfait's prologue. The scene illustrates Boccaccio's
own introduction to the first day, with an image of a stylized walled
rose garden within which two men and seven ladies listen to Panfilo, the
narrator of the first novella. The author sits outside the garden, faithfully
transcribing a scene he appears to witness first hand, in keeping with his
claim not to have invented his narrative. In this respect the image places
the *Decameron* alongside Boccaccio's compendious Latin works in which he
similarly acts as a compiler, rather than inventor of his material (Fig. 25).

The Italian *Decameron* manuscript acquired from the Holkham Hall
estate of the earls of Leicester (Oxford, Bodleian Library, MS. Holkham
misc. 49) is of an entirely different order to other early Italian *Decameron*
manuscripts; it in fact is one of the earliest extant copies from outside the
mercantile Florentine ambit.[48] It was produced on splendid parchment
by a professional team of scribe and artist for the court of Borso d'Este
(1413–71) in Ferrara; it was intended specifically for Borso's favourite,
Teofilo Calcagnini, whose badge and motto appear twice, at the start of
the introduction and the tenth day (fols. 5r and 148r, respectively). The
decoration, which can be attributed to the well-known illuminator Taddeo
Crivelli and to the year 1467 through the records of Borso's agents, is lavish
in its use of rich colours and gold leaf; but the images are disappointingly

Comincia il libro chiamato decameron
cognominato prencipe galeotto nel qua
le si contengono cento novelle in dieci
di dette da sette donne e da tre giovani
huomini. Proemio :—

Umana
cosa è il
vere com
passione
adglia f
flitti e
come che
ad ciascheduna per
sona sta
bene ad
coloro maximamente ne richiesto liquali
gia anno di conforto mestier auto et ilo
lo trovato in alcuni. fra ghliquali se alcu
no mai nebbe bisogno o glifu caro e
gia ne ricevette piacere. io sono uno di que
gli percio che dalla mia prima giovanezza
insino ad questo tempo oltre amodo essen
to stato acceso da altissimo et nobile amo
re forse piu assai chella mia bassa condi
tione non parrebbe narrandolo io sichie
desse quantunque appo coloro che discre
ti erano. et alla cui notitia pervenne io re
fossi lodato et da molto piu reputato non
dimeno mi fu egli di grandissima fatica
ad sofferire. Certo non per crudelta de
la donna amata ma per soperchio amo
re nella mente concepto da poco regola
appetito ilquale percio camino convene
vole termine mi lascia contento star piu
di noia che bisogno nomera ispesse volte
sentire mi faceva. Nella qual noia
tanto refriggerio mi porsono i piacevoli
ragionamenti dalcuno amico et lesue
laudevoli consolationi chello porto fortis
sima oppinione per quello essere adve
nuto che non sia morto. Ma si come
ad colui piacque ilquale essendo egli il
nito diede per legge incomutabile ad
tutte le cose mondane avere fine. Il mio
amore oltre ognialtro ferventemente et
ilquale niuna forza di proponimento
o di consiglio o divergogna evidente o
pericolo che seguir nepotesse avea potuto
nerompere nepiegare perse medesime in

processo di tempo si diminui in guisa che so
lo dise nellanimo m'ha al presente. lasciato
quel piacere che usato di porgere ad chi trop
po non simette ne suoi piu chupi pelaghi
navicando per che dove faticoso essere solea
ogni affanno toghliendo via dilectevole isen
to essere rimaso ma quantunque cessata
sia la pena non percio e la memoria fuggi
ta debemi sia gia ricevuti datui da coloro di
quali per benivolença da coloro ad me por
tata. Erano gravi le mie fatiche ne passera
mai si come credo senon per morte. Et pero
chella gratitudine secondo chio credo sia dal
le virtu e sommamente da comendare e ilcon
trario da biasimare per non parere ingrato
o meco stesso proposto di volere inquel poco
che per me si puo incambio di cio chio ricevetti
ora che libero dire mi possi et se non ad coloro
che me ataron alliquali peraventura per lo
loro seno o per la loro buona ventura non be
sogni ad quegli almeno aliquali fa luogo al
cuno alleggiamento prestare. Et quantun
que il mio sostentamento o conforto che vo
gliamo dire possa essere et sia abisognosi assai
poco. Nondimeno parmi quello doversi piu
tosto porgere dove il bisogno apparisce magio
re. si che piu utilita usfara et anchora pe
piu insia cara avuto. Et chi neghera que
sto quantunque egli si sia non molto piu alle
vaghe donne che ad glihuomini convenirsi do
nare. Et se dentro advilita petti temendo et
vergognando tenghono lamorose fiame na
scose lequali quanto piu siei forzi sieno della
palesi coloro ilsanno che lano provato et pro
vano. Et oltre advcio ristrette davoleri da
piaceri da comandamenti de padri delle ma
dri de fratelli et de mariti in picciol tempo nel
loro circhuito delle loro camere racchiuse di
morano et quasi oziose sedentosi volendo
et non volendo in una medesimo hora seco m
volgono diversi pensieri. liquali non e pos
sibile che sempre strano allegri. Esse per
quello mossa da focoso disio alcuna malinco
nia sopraviene nelle loro menti inquelle
conviene che con grave noia si dimori se da
nuovi ragionamenti non e rimossa sança
chelle sono molto meno forti che glihuomini
advsostenere. ilche degli innamorati huomini
non advviene si come noi possiamo apertame
te vedere essi se alcuna malinconia o gravezza

S. MARIA NOVELA

27.
Boccaccio, *Filocolo*, produced
for Ludovico II Gonzaga
in Mantua (1463–64).
Juno descending to talk to
Pope Clement IV. Oxford,
Bodleian Library, MS.
Canon. Ital. 85, fol 1r.

bland in comparison with the lively Italian visualizations of the early copies
described above. They consist of ten historiated initials depicting the bust
of the member of the *brigata* who 'rules' each day, with little differentiation
except of gender and with no characterization, although this is present in
the text. The miniature under the Proemio (fol. 5r) is far more elaborate,
purporting to show a cut-away interior of Santa Maria Novella, where
Boccaccio's storytellers meet. It is painted as if carved into the wall either
side of the semi-domed apse. Although the architecture is closer in spirit
to Alberti's Renaissance façade (completed some three years after this
manuscript) than to the Gothic church which Boccaccio would have known,
the miniature does demonstrate good textual knowledge (Fig. 26). It shows
a young lady, Pampinea, approaching three young men who join her and her
friends to form the storytelling *brigata*. This textual knowledge is put to scant
use thereafter, and the images once again serve as embellishment and textual
markers, rather than as genuine illustrations designed to aid or influence
understanding of the text. They do, however, establish a tone of courtly
elegance in keeping with the circulation of the manuscript – if not with the
tone of Boccaccio's Introduction recounting the horrors of the plague in
Florence, nor the tenor of the frequently bawdy tales, many of which are set
in far more modest circles. The tone of the latter is only faithfully captured
in manuscripts which include fuller programmes of illustration and depict
the contents of the tales themselves.

The images found in two more illustrated Boccaccio manuscripts seem
more appropriate to the texts they visualize. The sumptuous miniatures
contained within the luxurious *Filocolo* manuscript[49] produced in the
Gonzaga court at Mantua in 1463–64 do match the tone of Boccaccio's text,
which is an Italian prose version of the French romance *Fleur et Blanchfleur*.
The story appeared in Italy at approximately the same time (*c.* 1336–39) as
the humbler *Cantare di Fiorio e Biancifiore*, but Boccaccio's narrative, with its
prologue set in Angevin Naples, lifts the fable from its modest origins.
The manuscript was copied by Andrea da Lodi for Ludovico II Gonzaga
(1444–78), whose arms are contained in the border decoration of each
of the five folios that include miniatures.[50] These miniatures, which have
been attributed to Pietro Guindaleri, and are close in style to works by
more famous artists such as Mantegna, Cossa and Tura, illustrate scenes
from each of the five books they precede with some accurate textual detail,
although they do not uniformly suggest a good grasp of the text. The
opening illustration, depicting Juno descending on her peacock-drawn
chariot to visit Pope Clement IV (who at her bidding summons to Italy the
dynasty of Angevin kings, beginning with Charles of Anjou) is perhaps the
most accurate and simultaneously the most revealing. Juno's descent, which
echoes the opening of the *Aeneid*, hitches Boccaccio's first major vernacular
prose work to the classical tradition, while the illustration shows a scene that

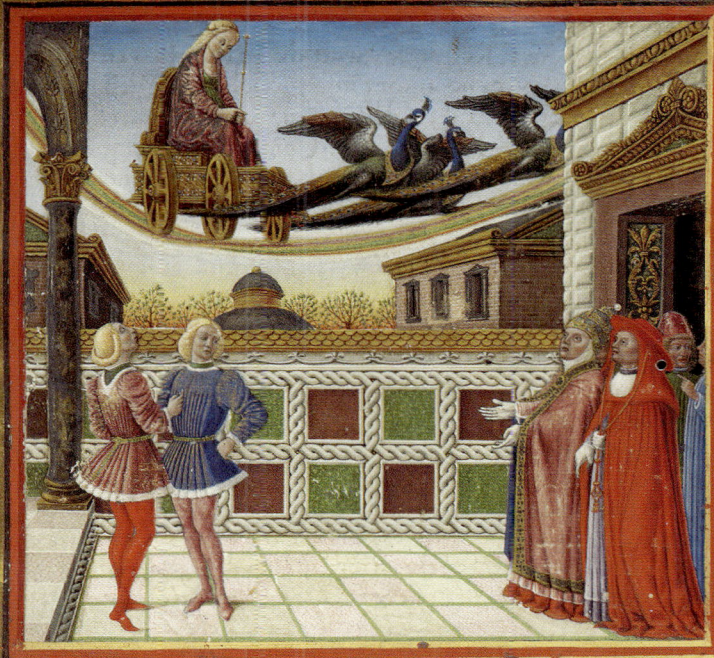

ANCAE GIA
TANTO LE FORSE
DEL VALOROSO
POPOLO ANTICA

mente discesa del
troiano enea che qu
asi al mente uenute
erano per lo mara
uiglioso ualore di
Iunone la quale la
morte della pactoui
ta didone cartagine
se non auea uoluta

multa dimenticare. et allaltre offese porte non debita dimen
ticanga facendo delli antiqui peccati de padri sostenere a fi

28.
Boccaccio, *Filocolo*, produced
for Ludovico II Gonzaga in
Mantua (1463-64). Florio
(Filocolo) and companions
set off from Marmorina
(Verona) in search of
Biancifiore on horseback
since the sea is too rough.
Oxford, Bodleian Library,
MS. Canon. Ital. 85, fol.
114v.

would undoubtedly appeal to the dynastic patron of this manuscript (Fig.
27).[51] By contrast, the illustration at the start of Book 4 actually depicts the
final scene from Book 3, where the hero Filocolo sets off from Marmorina
(Verona), in the company of his friends, in search of his beloved (Fig. 28).

Like the *Decameron*, Boccaccio's *Filostrato* (the romance of Troilus and
Criseide, written around 1334) had its initial readership in bourgeois
Florentine circles. Its early manuscript tradition, therefore, makes little
provision for rich decoration or extensive illustration. Where there are
illustrations, for example in Florence, Biblioteca Nazionale Centrale, MS. II
II 90, they are again lively narrative scenes sketched in pen and ink. As the
text circulated more widely, however, the manuscripts were heavily influenced
by the prevailing style of the circles into which they were introduced. This
is clear from an example of the *Roman de Troyle* (Oxford, Bodleian Library,
MS. Douce 331), a mid-fifteenth-century French translation of Boccaccio's
work. This was made almost undoubtedly by Louis de Beauveau, sometime
Seneschal of Anjou, who perhaps became familiar with Boccaccio's work
while resident in the Neapolitan court of King René between 1438 and 1442.
Datable *c.* 1480, MS. Douce 331 belonged to the d'Albret family, seigneurs of
Orval (in what was then Burgundy). The ten courtly miniatures it contains
all occur on folios with fully decorated borders and make extensive use
of rich colours, including gold, thus firmly placing the manuscript in the
luxurious category, despite the relatively poor artistry of the visualizations.
These come at fairly regular intervals and all correspond to the placing
of rubrics in the Italian texts, but not with the major divisions of the
text. Although the characters and settings of the stories have been given a
contemporary French look and focus almost exclusively upon the romance
narrative, the visualizations are all close to the text, itself a faithful prose
rendition of Boccaccio's verse. This can be seen in the image on fol. 26r,
where the lovers meet and the symbolic flames of passion are visualized by
the textually accurate inclusion of a burning candle (Fig. 29).

The history of early printed editions of Boccaccio's work has several
parallels with the manuscript tradition. Once again the importance of the
Latin texts to Boccacio's reputation is clear, as is the manner in which both
Latin and Italian works were often lavishly illustrated by the end of the
fifteenth century. Indeed, Boccaccio's works proved extremely popular as
printed editions, illustrated ones in particular.[52] The 1470s saw editions of
virtually all of his works, with Florence and Venice leading the way in their
production. At first they tended to be in the language in which they were
originally written, but translations of the Latin works into Italian and other
European languages soon followed.

The first illustrated edition of one of Boccaccio's works was also the
first edition of *De mulieribus*, printed in 1473 in Ulm by Johann Zainer.
This was soon after the first known appearance in print of any of the

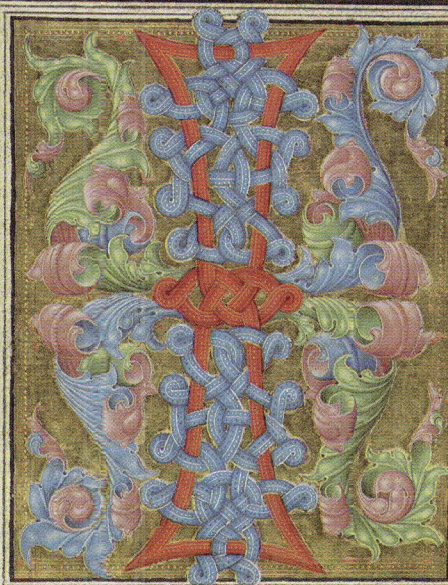

dolore sollicita li
passi de compagni
seguendo quelli de
Ascalion amaestratis
simo duca dell.o
camino Ma sfati
da non potere fugre
uolfero in arco la
directa uia Et prim
eramente uenuti ala
gugosa terra oue ti

manto crudissima giouane lisciò le sue ossi con eterno nome
passarono oltre per lo piaceuole piano Ma poi che dietr.o

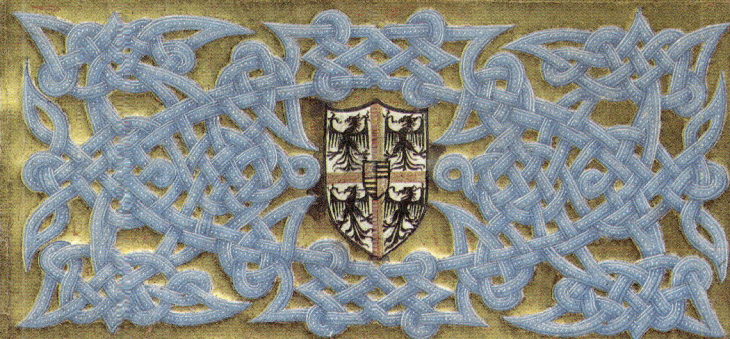

29.
Boccaccio, *Filostrato*, French
translation by Louis de
Beauveau (1438–42),
manuscript *c.* 1480. Oxford,
Bodleian Library, MS.
Douce 331, fol 26r.

author's works, a 1470 copy of the *Decameron*, probably produced in Naples. Although editions of Boccaccio's vernacular works appeared very quickly north of the Alps, it is noteworthy that it was once again a Latin work which had priority; and it proved widely popular, as further editions of the *De mulieribus* appeared in Strasbourg (*c.* 1474–5) and Louvain (1487). Translations of this and other Latin works soon followed: Zainer published a German translation of *De mulieribus* in the same year as his Latin edition; and French (Paris, 1493), Spanish (Saragossa, 1494), and eventually Italian (Venice, 1506) translations were also printed. Meanwhile, *De casibus* was published in Strasbourg in 1474–75, an illustrated French translation came out in Bruges in 1476, and an illustrated English edition of Lydgate's *Fall of Princes* was printed in London in 1494.

The woodcuts in these early editions generally demonstrate good textual understanding, and were of such high artistic quality that many blocks were used or re-used as the models for subsequent editions. In terms of their content and their position within the text, the images are very similar in style to the miniatures of the later manuscript tradition, by which they obviously were influenced. The opening page was typically the most ornate, including a full border or larger illustration. This is exemplified by the first page of a copy of Jacopo Foresti da Bergamo's adaptation of *De mulieribus* printed in Ferrara in 1497.[53] Illustrations also tend to appear at major divisions of the work, such as at the start of each book of the London *Fall of Princes* (Fig. 30).[54] Illustrations often appear at smaller textual divisions also, for example the woodcuts of Sappho and Lucretia in the Ulm and Louvain editions of *De mulieribus* (Fig. 31).[55] In these cases the woodcuts usually present vignettes which summarize the ensuing text, imitating the role played by rubrics in both manuscripts and editions.

Although numerous editions of the *Decameron* prove it was probably the most-read Italian work of the late fifteenth century, its first illustrated edition was printed in Paris by Jean Dupré in 1485, using the same woodcut for the start of each day. The first fully illustrated edition also appeared outside Italy: a German translation printed by Anton Sorg in Augsburg in 1490, it contains a programme of illustration clearly influenced by the Ulm *De mulieribus*. Not until 1492 was an illustrated Italian edition finally published by Giovanni e Gregorio de' Gregori in Venice.[56] This Venetian edition is now very rare, with only seven known surviving copies. Nevertheless it proved to be a highly influential model for subsequent editions of the *Decameron*. Like the non-Italian productions, it looks very similar to the editions of Boccaccio's Latin works and to the later and more

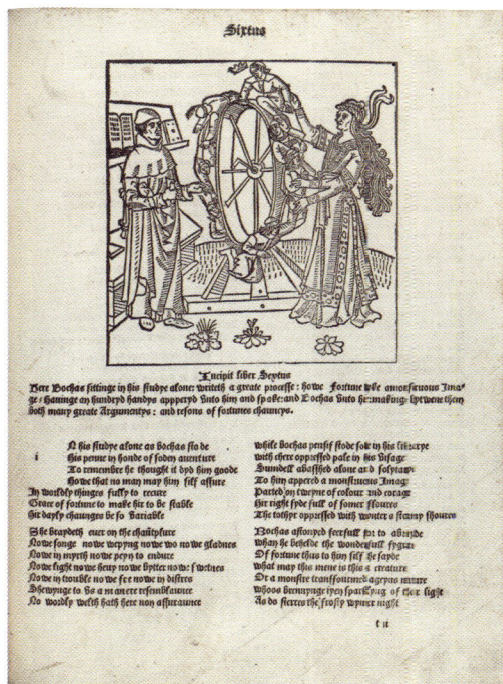

30.
Lydgate, *Fall of Princes* (London: Richard Pynson, 1494), start of Book 6: Boccas and the Wheel of Fortune. Oxford, Bodleian Library, Arch G. d.26.

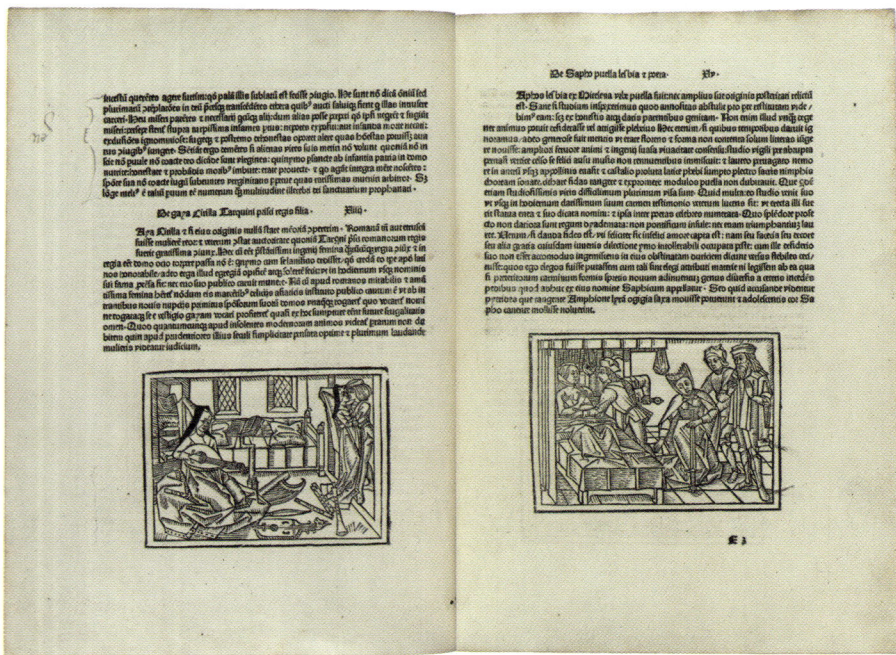

luxurious Italian and French manuscripts, or at least those with numerous illustrations of the *novelle* themselves. It contains woodcuts for each *novella*, as well as an author portrait, a frontispiece of the *brigata* and two different images for the days presided over by ladies and by men, used at the start of each day. The frontispiece makes an interesting comparison with both the images from the Bodleian manuscripts, as it contains a condensed scene of the meeting in Santa Maria Novella, as well as a central image of the *brigata* seated in a *hortus conclusus* (Fig. 32).

The 1492 edition is technically very fine, and it skilfully summarizes the tales with great economy, often using a bipartite division of space to show different moments of each narrative. Its lively scenes remind us why it was ultimately the *Decameron* which secured Boccaccio's fame in later centuries, appearing in innumerable editions and translations, such as the 1725 London reprint of a 1527 Florentine edition which had as many as three author portraits[57] and the Navarre Society edition of 1922 with plates by Louis Chalon.[58]

Boccaccio is usually placed third among Italy's Three Crowns for chronological reasons, and also because his works had less resonance in European culture compared with the pervasive influence of Dante and Petrarch. Nevertheless, the strong narrative drive in most of his works meant that they were particularly amenable to visual illustration, to which the sumptuous quality of Oxford's best Boccaccio manuscripts bears eloquent testimony.

VMANA COSA ELHAVER COMPASSIONE
A GLI AFFLITTI. e come che a ciaschuna psona ftia
bene a choloro maffimaméte e richiefto liquali gia há
no di conforto hauuto misteri: & hánolo trouato in al
cuno fra liquali fe alcuno mai nebbe:ogli fu caro o gia
ne riceuete piacere .Io fono uno di quelli p cio che dal
la mia prima giouenezza infino a questo tempo :oltra
modo effendo ftato accefo da altiffimo & nobile amo
re forfe piu affai chella mia baffa conditione non pare
be narrandolo io fi richiedeffe: quantunque doppo
coloro che difcreti erano: & alla cui noticia puéne:io ne fuffi lodato & da mol
to piu reputato. Non dimeno mi fu egli di grádiffima fatica a foffrire:certo
non per crudelta della donna amata:ma per fouecrhio amore nella mente con
cepto da pocho regolato appetito .ilquale percio a niuno regolato cóueneuo
le termine milafcia contento ftare piu di noia che di bifogno nó era fpeffe uol
te fentire mi faceua. Nella qual noia tanto refrigerio mi porfero li piaceuoli
ragionamenti dalcuno amico & le delecteuole fue cófolatióe che io porto fer

CHAPTER 4

Dante's reception in fifteenth- and sixteenth-century Italy

Simon A. Gilson

In the fifteenth and sixteenth centuries, despite Petrarch's humanist revolution, the influence of Dante's *Commedia* was felt at almost all levels of Italian society and in all the main geographical areas. Diffused throughout the peninsula both in manuscript and (from the 1470s onwards) in print, the poem is read by merchants, artisans, and artists, as well as by courtiers, princes, and popes. It is quoted in sermons delivered by preachers in public squares and lectured upon by jurists, theologians, and even some humanists in crowded churches and lecture-halls. It is held up as a wellspring of the Italian language and acts as a constant point of reference in Italian poetry, being handled in the most varied manner, at times with reverential awe, at others in audaciously bawdy parody. The authoritative status of Dante's poem is confirmed and enhanced by being translated into Latin and receiving learned commentary, in both Latin and the vernacular; its presence can even be detected in some neo-Latin poetry. It is mined for its encyclopaedic range of scientific and philosophical content: 'Dante is a knave because he has said everything, and has left nothing for others to say', commented one mercantile reader in the mid-1440s. Dante is himself an object of attention from a variety of perspectives: anecdotes tell of his uncompromising moral stature and his mordant wit; biographies reconstruct his life from varying ideological standpoints; the visual arts establish him as a visual type in his own right and illustrate his representations of the afterlife.[59]

The history of how Dante is critically refashioned and the *Commedia* emerges as a vernacular 'classic' involves a complex series of pressures and contestations as later readers judge and re-shape his cultural authority as poet and intellectual. Such re-readings take place in conjunction with major landmarks in Italian cultural history in the fifteenth and sixteenth centuries: the rise and development of humanism; the history of the Italian language; the coming of print culture; the promotion of Florentine and

Italian identity; the Reform movement, the Counter-Reformation, and the Inquisition. Perhaps the single most important theme – one already evident in some of the first commentators – is Dante's relationship with classical antiquity. The view that Dante marks a pivotal moment in the revival of classical poetry and learning, that his *Commedia* had in effect brought 'dead poetry from the darkness to the light', is first stated in the mid-1330s.[60] And yet, for a culture that, especially from the late fourteenth century onwards, was becoming increasingly dominated by Latin and ever more conscious of the need to imitate classical standards, Dante's choice of the vernacular for his poem could not be easily digested. Perhaps unsurprisingly, it was Francesco Petrarca (1304–74), so keenly intent upon establishing his own foundational role in reviving Latin letters, who led the way. As we saw in Chapter 2, in his celebrated 1359 Latin letter – *Familiares* 21.15 ('Letters on Familiar Matters', 1359) – Petrarch had implicitly denied that Dante had brought about a rebirth of classical learning, and subtly diminished the *Commedia*'s cultural value, by emphasizing the superiority of the ancients over the moderns and of literary production in Latin over that in the vernacular. Many of Dante's later humanist readers were also startled by his promotion of the vernacular, and troubled by the unclassical qualities of Dante's own scholastic Latin, as well as by deficiencies in his knowledge of antiquity. In the *Commedia*, for example, Dante has Virgil born under the wrong emperor and erroneously claims that the Latin poet Statius was a native of Toulouse. In this chapter we will explore various facets of Dante's critical and textual history in the fifteenth and sixteenth centuries, paying particular attention to the highly differentiated humanist reception, to Florentine concerns to make political and ideological capital out of his name and works, and to the *Commedia*'s growing – yet often contested and qualified – status as a vernacular classic in later Renaissance Italy.

By 1400 Florence in particular had seized upon the potential to exploit Dante's name and the cult of the *Commedia* in order to enhance the city's reputation. The tradition of public readings of Dante – inaugurated by Giovanni Boccaccio (1313–75) in late October 1373 – was well established. Thanks in large part to the efforts of Boccaccio, too, a cult of the poet Dante, one already shrouded in myth and legend, had taken a vigorous hold. Calls were being made for his remains to be returned from Ravenna, and he was emerging as a visual object for public consumption in commissions for Florence's cathedral and for fresco cycles in major civic buildings. Dante had, in short, become a primary object of Florentine civic pride, especially amongst those Tuscan literati who, from the 1380s, were members of the ruling oligarchy and were active in the city as notaries, teachers, and scholars.

The decades around 1400 see Florence at the vanguard of attempts to recover ancient letters and civilization with discoveries of classical works, new techniques of textual philology, closer imitation of classical Latin, and the recovery of the language and cultural heritage of ancient Greece. Various efforts are made in Florence to tailor Dante to such preoccupations, on the one hand, and to distance him from them, on the other. That some sections of the early humanist movement rebelled against the cult of Dante is clear from the tone of strident polemic taken by his defenders in the late 1390s and early 1400s. A wealthy Florentine merchant and founder of an important school of rhetoric, Cino Rinuccini (1350–1417), for example, viciously lampoons the humanists, sets up Dante as surpassing all poets, both Greek and Latin, including Virgil, and even maintains that the vernacular is more concise, more adaptable, and more authoritative than Latin.[61] One of Rinuccini's principal antagonists is Niccolò Niccoli (1364–1437), a militant classicist who seems to have sought a complete break with the vernacular legacy of the Trecento.

In the 1390s the first humanist chancellor of the city, Coluccio Salutati (1332–1406), also becomes a strenuous, though more subtle, defender of Dante, as he responds to a younger generation of humanists, including Niccoli, and to two later humanist chancellors, Leonardo Bruni (1370–1444) and Poggio Bracciolini (1380–1459), who perceived Dante's use of the vernacular, his Latin style, and many of his teachings as remote from their own interests and values. While Salutati expresses some reservations about Dante's choice of the vernacular, he nonetheless associates him with the ancients in terms of his knowledge and inventiveness. Salutati is unwilling to jettison the distinctive legacy of Florence's vernacular literary culture, as embodied by the 'Three Crowns'– Dante, Petrarch, and Boccaccio. To affirm Dante's excellence is, he observes in a late Latin letter (1406), to claim literary and cultural primacy for Florence; to treat him lightly is to 'take away from the reputation of our city'.[62] Salutati also defends, in his *De tyranno* ('On Tyranny', *c.*1400), another increasingly sensitive aspect of Dante's legacy, the poet's political views – especially his overriding conviction that the Roman Empire was divinely preordained, and his condemnation, in *Inferno* XXXIV, of Brutus and Cassius as treacherous assassins of Julius Caesar. Such sentiments were not easily reconciled with the intense local patriotism and strong Republican sentiments of the Florentine state in the closing decades of the fourteenth century. The Florentine Republic now viewed Brutus and Cassius as heroic figures, and tended to condemn Caesar's position of personal power as emperor in the Roman Republic.

Against this background emerges the most fascinating document in the early affirmation of the humanist movement in Florence and its complex negotiation with Dante's legacy – Leonardo Bruni's *Dialogi ad Petrum Paulum Histrum* ('Dialogues to Pier Paolo Vergerio', *c.* 1404–6). In Book I the character Niccolò Niccoli supports his general argument about the moribund state of classical learning in contemporary Florence by demonstrating the specific deficiencies of the Three Crowns in classical matters. Dante was a bad interpreter of Virgil, and he anachronistically referred to Cato of Utica as an old man. Worse still, he had unfairly condemned Brutus, the just assassin of the tyrant Caesar. Dante was ignorant of Latin letters, and wrote clumsily in Latin, since he was influenced by his reading of the scholastic treatises of friars. Some earlier criticisms of Dante's lesser abilities as a Latinist had been voiced by Petrarch, Boccaccio, and Salutati, but what is extraordinary here is the full-scale diatribe against Dante's ignorance of Latin language and culture. In Book II Niccoli offers a retraction, but the specific criticisms of Dante's lack of classical knowledge are not strictly withdrawn, and the general points about his inelegant Latin and medieval scholastic interests remain unanswered, and are reiterated even in Bruni's later biography of the poet. By contrast, Petrarch is singled out as opening up the pathway towards the *studia humanitatis*. Bruni, as author of the *Dialogi*, may thus react against the extreme position of the historical Niccoli and rehabilitate Dante in Book II, but he does not bestow upon him the cultural centrality that had been stressed by other Florentines.

In the 1430s the battle-lines in the struggle over Dante take on a still more ideological tincture. Particularly revealing are the public readings (1429–34) of Dante in Florence by the Tolentine humanist Francesco Filelfo (1398–1481). In a climate of heated rivalries as the Medici jostle for power against the ruling oligarchy, Filelfo uses his orations to place Dante above the ancients and praise the universal appeal of his vernacular eloquence. In this way he aligns himself with the traditionalist vision of Dante that is pre-eminently associated with the cultural patrimony of the pre-Medici oligarchy. In other orations, Filelfo imbues Dante with all the values of civic patriotism associated with the Republican oligarchy. In other words, Dante has become a politically charged symbol at a time of tumultuous factional rivalry. The Medici respond by sponsoring a campaign to remove Filelfo from his posts at the university and even hiring an assailant to disfigure him with a knife.

The 1430s see other ideologized attempts — albeit less turbulent and bloody — to use Dante's name in order to justify specific forms of civic patriotism. Matteo Palmieri (1406–75) takes Dante's participation at the Battle of Campaldino (11 June 1289) as the basis for his portrait of him as the archetypal civic patriot in the final book of his vernacular dialogue, the *Vita civile* ('On Civic Life', *c.* 1433–36). But the most complex treatment is Leonardo Bruni's *Vita di Dante* ('Life of Dante') of May 1436. In this biography of the poet, Bruni develops almost all the principal motifs of Florentine patriotism and Republican ideology in the first third of the fifteenth century. Shot through with explicit polemic against the way Boccaccio had emphasized Dante's amorous dalliances in his Dante biography of the 1360s, Bruni eliminates all mention of love affairs and adopts a tone of historicizing circumspection throughout. Elaborating an ideology of the Florentine citizen that owes much to his keen interest in Aristotle and Cicero, Bruni's Dante is a true man of action, fighting for his homeland at Campaldino, taking a wife, and immersing himself in city politics. Bruni also praises Dante's use of the vernacular, but such a linguistic choice is put down to Dante's own recognition of his greater ability in this language rather than in Latin; and the legitimacy of the vernacular poetic tradition seems only to be recognized within certain contexts. Some thirty years on from the *Dialogi*, then, Bruni uses the *Vita di Dante* to refashion a portrait of Dante as a civic humanist, but his comments on Dante's abilities in Latin prose and verse recycle his own earlier criticisms as well as those of Petrarch in the 1359 letter.

In the 1440s and 1450s humanists in Florence and elsewhere continue to devalue the vernacular. Only from the 1460s onwards do we witness the first stirrings of a renewed movement in Florence towards employing the vernacular at higher cultural levels. Lorenzo de' Medici (1449–92), who effectively assumes power in 1469, plays a key role in intensifying efforts to promote the Tuscan vernacular by linking it to the political standing and intellectual prestige of the Florentine state. The late 1460s and 1470s witness various initiatives that attempt to recover the vernacular tradition. Cristoforo Landino (1425–98), professor of rhetoric and poetry at the Florentine university, defends the vernacular as a language which can be ennobled and perfected through study of Latin models and their transposition into the vernacular. In 1468 Marsilio Ficino (1433–99), the great translator of Plato, produces his own vernacular version of Dante's Latin treatise on world politics *Monarchia* (1317–18), at a time when conflict between Medici Florence and the papacy gave new significance to Dante's view that papal authority should rest with spiritual matters, and temporal authority should be concentrated in a single secular ruler. Vernacular versions are also made of Latin and Greek works, and an important collection of Italian poetry – the so-called *Raccolta Aragonese* ('The Aragon Collection', 1476–77), produced by Angelo Poliziano (1454–94) – is collated and edited with philological acumen for the first time.

Amidst the vernacular ferment in Florence that sees Dante's presence growing at higher cultural levels and in strongly politicized contexts, the printing press arrives in Italy. It soon becomes clear that Dante is far from being an exclusively Florentine phenomenon. The first printed edition of Dante is produced in Foligno in 1472 by Johann Numeister, in a format that reveals close continuities with the manuscript tradition by its use of abbreviations and brief arguments before each canticle and canto (Fig. 33). The *editio princeps* is followed by further printings in Venice and Milan in 1472, and then by five more between 1477 and 1478 in Venice, Naples,

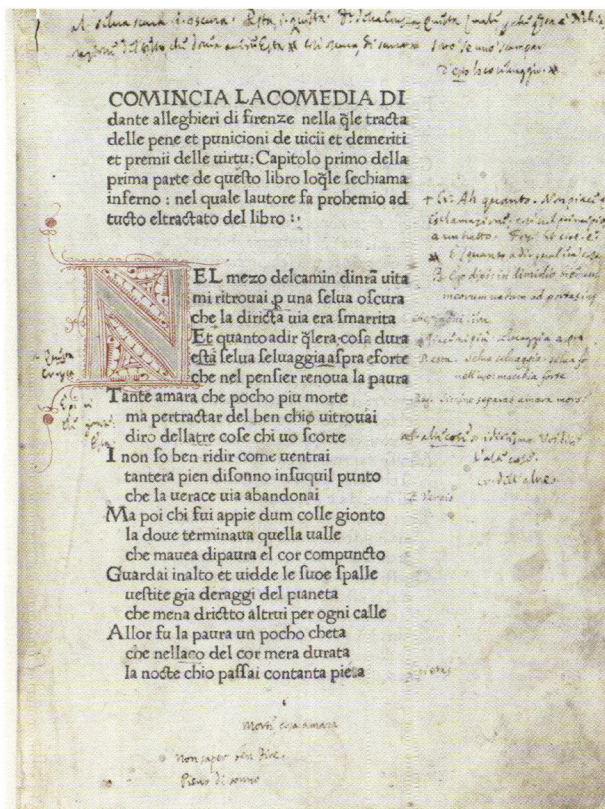

33.
First page of *Inferno* in the Foligno *editio princeps* of Dante's *Comedia* (1472). Oxford, Bodleian Library, Auct. 2Q 2.18, first page.

and Milan. The geographical range of these printings demonstrates the popularity of Dante's poem in the peninsula and its emerging status as an Italian classic. Along with Dante's text one finds earlier commentaries being reprinted, such as Jacopo della Lana's Bolognese commentary (*c.* 1324–28), first in the Venetian edition of 1477, and, more significantly, in the 1478 Milanese edition prepared by Martino Paolo Nibia or Nidobeato. Nidobeato's edition is notable in its own right for interventions in historical and political matters, where it updates Lana and revitalizes the *Commedia*, bringing it into line with the vernacular tastes of a readership based in the northern courts, and allowing humanistic culture there to enter into fertile contact with the literary tradition of the Trecento.

Goaded by Nidobeato, who had challenged the pre-eminence of Tuscan in the preface to his edition, Cristoforo Landino – by now Florence's best-known teacher of Dante – prepared the first new printed commentary in 1480–81. The *Comento di Christophoro Landino Fiorentino sopra la Comedia di Danthe Alighieri poeta fiorentino* (printed by Niccolò Tedesco on 30 August 1481) was to become the most famous and influential Renaissance printed edition. Landino's *Comento* is made up of two distinct sections which have quite different purposes: a lengthy prologue that celebrates Dante as the supreme

EL
ME
ZO
DEL
CA
MI
NO
DI
NO
ST
RA
VI
TA

h abbiamo narrato non solamente lauita del poeta et eltitolo dellibro et che cosa sia poeta Ma etiam quãto sia uetusta et antica quãto nobile et uaria quanto utile et ioconda tai doctrina. Quanto sia efficace a muouere lhumane meti; et quãto dilecti ogni liberale igegno. Ne giudicammo da tacere quanto in si diuina disciplina sia stata la excellentia dello ingegno del nostro poeta. Inche sisono stato piu brieue che forse non si conuerebbe; consideri chi legge che lanumerosa et quasi infinita copia dellecose delle quali e necessario tractare misforza non uolédo chel uolume cresca sopra modo; a inculcare et inuiluppare piutosto che explicare: et disedere moltecose et maxime quelle lequali quãdo ben tacessi non pero ne restera obscura la expositione del testo. Verremo adunque aquella. Ma perche stimo non esser lectore alcuno ne di si basso ingegno: ne di si pocho giudicio; che hauendo inteso; quanto sia et laprofondita et uarieta della doctrina; et la excellentia et diuinita dello ingegno delnostro toscano: et fiorentino poeta; non si persuada che questo principio delprimo canto debba per sublimita et grandeza esser pari alla stupenda doctrina dellecose che seguitano: pero con ogni industria in uesti gheremo che allegoricho senso arechi seco questo mezo, delcamino: et che cosa sia selua Diche ueggio non piccola differentia essere stata tra glinterpreti et expositori diquesta cantica. Im pero che alchuni dicono: che il mezo della uita humana e el sonno mossi; credo dalla sententia daristotele dicendo lui nellethica nessuna differentia essere tra felici: et miseri nella meta della uita per che lenocti che sono lameta del tempo cinducono sonno: et daquello nasce che ne bene nemale sentir possiamo. Ilperche uogliono questi: che el poeta pongha el mezo della uita per la nocte: e lanocte pelsonno; ad notare che questo poema non sia altro che una uisione che gliapparue dormédo per laquale hebbe cognitõe delle cose dallui descripte i queste tre comedie. Dicono adúque che lui imita Ioanni euangelista el

Mi ritrouai peruna selua obscura
che la dricta uita era smarrita
Et quanto adire quale era e/ cosa dura
esta selua seluaggia et aspra et forte
che nel pensier rinuoua lapaura
Tanto era amara che pocho e piu morte
ma per tractar del ben chio ui trouai
diro dellaltre cose chio uho scorte
I non so ben ridire chomio uentrai
tantera piena disonno insu quel puncto
che lauerace uia abbandonai
Ma pot chio fui appie dun colle giunto
la oue terminaua quella ualle
che mhauea dipaur el cor compuncto
Guardai inalto et uidi lesue spalle
coperte gia deraggi delpianeta
che mena dricto altrui per ogni calle
Allhor fu lapaura un pocho queta
che nellago del chuor mera durata
lanocte chio passai con tanta pieta

quale dormédo sopra elpecto di christo redemptore hebbe uisione delle chose celeste: oueraméte ponghi lanocte dimostrando lui hauere cominciato elsuo poema dinocte nella quale raccogliédosi lanimo insemedesimo et absoluendosi et liberandosi da ogni cura meglio intenda. Ma benche tale sententia quadri al poeta; nientedimeno leparole non la dimostrono senon cõ tanto obscura ambiguita; che non pare degna della elegantia ditanto poeta Prima perche nonseguita che benche nelle reuolutioni deltempo tanto spatio occupin lenocti quanto e di; perquesto dicendo io scripsi dinocte sintenda io scripsi nel mezo della mia eta; perche nel principio et nelfine della eta humana sono lenocti chome nel mezo et similmente e di. Il perche per lamedesima ragione si potrebbe fare tale interpretatione pel di chome per lanocte. Altridicono che uolle pelmezo del camino intendere che nelmezo delleta dette principio alsuo poema. Ma non e unamedsima opinione deltermine della nostra eta: per che diuersi scriptori diuersamente sentono. Aristotile nel suo de republica

embodiment of Florence's cultural traditions, and an extensive body of commentary in the form of glosses on all three canticles of the *Commedia*. At one level, the commentary is an attempt to reclaim Dante for the city. That this is, at least in part, a collective effort is shown by the collaboration of other Florentines in the prologue. Ficino provides a Latin letter that heralds Dante's symbolic return to the city between the covers of Landino's edition. Sandro Botticelli offered the original illustrations upon which is based the incomplete series of copperplate engravings or *intagli* – the first figurative cycle in a printing of Dante – to the first nineteen cantos of the *Inferno* (Fig. 34). A merchant copyist and cosmographer, Antonio Manetti (1423–97), provides the material for a chapter that deals with questions concerning the site and size of Dante's Hell, a line of enquiry that continues to interest readers well into the sixteenth century (Figs. 35, 36).[63]

Landino's patriotism is prominent in the prologue's opening chapter, where he speaks of his concern to 'liberate our citizen Dante from the barbarity of many foreign idioms', and to restore him to 'his homeland after long exile' in 'pure Florentine, a language which is greater than any other Italian idiom, as is shown clearly by the fact that no one ever expressed genius or doctrine nor wrote verses or prose, who did not attempt to use the Florentine idiom'.[64] Landino, like Lorenzo de' Medici, was deeply conscious of the political and cultural advantages that would accrue to Florence from widespread diffusion of Tuscan to other areas of Italy. The edition itself makes little progress in restoring Dante's text to its early Trecento form, although Landino's glosses provide an important body of observations on Dante's language and style. Much of the remainder of the prologue – after a defence of Dante in which he radically reconfigures the poet's own invectives against Florence – celebrates Florentine culture, its eloquent and learned citizens, its musicians, painters and sculptors, lawyers, and merchants. Somewhat more traditionally, Landino also finds space for his own life of Dante.

Not surprisingly, given Landino's concern with a humanistic refounding of the vernacular, a classicizing reading of Dante is a prominent feature of the *Comento*. In the prologue he emphasizes structural links between Virgil's *Aeneid* and Dante's *Commedia*: both poems are read as the journey of a man who follows the path towards perfection that ends in contemplation of divine ideas. There is no suggestion at all that Dante had little or no grounding in the Latin classics or that the vernacular operates on a lower level. Quite the opposite; unlike both Homer and Virgil, who found their languages already polished, ornate, and abundant, Landino

34.
Inferno, opening page with engraved illustration in Cristoforo Landino, *Comento sopra la Comedia* (Florence: Niccolò Tedesco, 1481). Oxford, Bodleian Library, Auct. 2Q 1.11, opening page.

35.
Map of Hell and Purgatory in Girolamo Benivieni, *Commedia di Dante insieme con uno dialogo circa al sito, forma et misure dello Inferno* (Florence: Filippo Giunta, 1506). Oxford, Taylorian Library, 101.C.15 (Dialogo only), opening map.

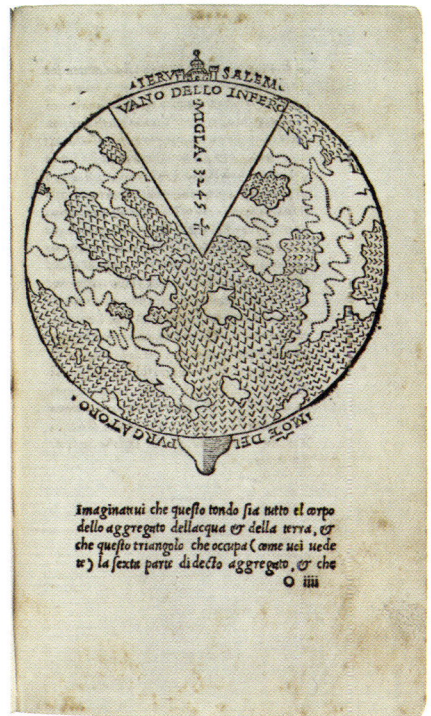

IEPVS ALEM

M SION

SCIAGVRATI

LIMBO

CARNALI

GOLOSI

PRODIGHI ET AVARI

IRACVNDI ET ACCIDIOSE

HERESIARCHI

VIOLENTI

FRAVDOL
ENTI

TRADITORI

LVCIFERO

sees Dante as establishing an elegant and refined literary language almost without any vernacular precedents. His foundational role is, moreover, the result of his close familiarity with the Latin tradition and his imitation of that tradition in Tuscan. Long before Coleridge fêted Shakespeare as myriad-minded, Landino hails Dante as the pinnacle of learning and eloquence: 'O immortal God, what a genius! What a profound mind. He [Dante] encompasses Heaven, Earth, and the Tartarean realm.'[65]

In the commentary proper Landino performs many of the functions found in the earlier tradition of Trecento Dante commentary with which he was closely familiar. He provides his readers with a substantial body of literary instruction and encyclopaedic teaching. He makes extensive use of paraphrase. He repeatedly engages in linguistic, rhetorical, and etymological analysis. He develops lengthy digressions on matters of ancient and modern history, geography and natural lore, philosophy and theology, law, mythology, music, and many other topics. Landino shows a strong interest in using allegorical reading to interpret the *Commedia*, but he is unusual in doing this on a philosophical plane and in close connection with his understanding of Virgil's Latin epic as the ascent of the mind from sensuality to the contemplation of God. Recent studies of Landino's *Comento* have shown that, although it is closely connected to the earlier commentary tradition, his glosses are very much alive to contemporary Florentine and Italian discussions of doctrine, science, and the ancient world. Of particular note are the insertions – over eighty in total – Landino makes concerning Plato and Platonic writers, often as the basis for his allegorized readings.

36.
Frontispiece with map of Hell in Bernardino Daniello, *L'Espositione di Bernardino Daniello da Lucca sopra la Comedia di Dante* (Venice: Pietro da Fino, 1568). Oxford, Bodleian Library, 4° D 2 Art, frontispiece.

The popularity of Landino's commentary was remarkable. It was one of the most reprinted and widely read humanist books in Renaissance Italy, not least because it acted as a kind of *summa* of earlier Dante commentary and provided a wealth of doctrinal material. Even after the publication of new sixteenth-century commentaries by Alessandro Vellutello (sixteenth century) and Bernardino Daniello (*c.* 1500–65), Landino's work continued to be reprinted both on its own and alongside Vellutello's commentary, first published in 1544, in Francesco Sansovino's Venetian editions of 1564, 1578, and 1596 (Fig. 37). Print plays an important role in further raising Dante's reputation in Italy and helping

37.
Title-page of 1564 Sansovino Venetian edition of the *Commedia*, with commentaries by Landino and Vellutello. Oxford, Taylorian Library, ARCH. FOL.IT.1564(1)

him to acquire a trans-Alpine dimension. The sixteenth century sees the *Commedia* presented in a gamut of sizes and page designs, often preceded by tables of notable matters and accompanied by printed illustrations: folio editions surround his text with commentary (sometimes more than one), whereas portable volumes offer Dante without commentary to readers in courts and towns. Venice becomes a centre for such initiatives, and amidst other innovations in the production of 'Dantes', the epithet 'divina' was added to the title page, in the 1555 Venetian edition prepared by Lodovico Dolce (1508–68) (Fig. 9.).

If the beginning of the fifteenth century saw a provocation from Florentine humanists, the beginning of the sixteenth is witness to a subtler refashioning of Dante in print by the Venetian humanist and courtier Pietro Bembo (1470–1547). The edition in question is the 1502 octavo printed by Aldus Manutius (1449–1515) after a text transcribed by Bembo and based upon a fourteenth-century manuscript – once given by Boccaccio to Petrarch

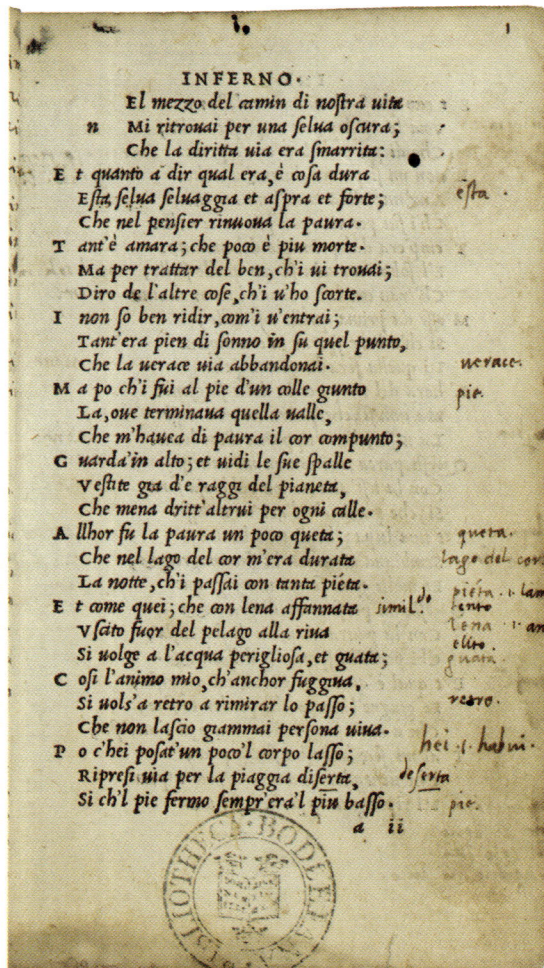

38.
Opening page of *Inferno*, in Bembo's Aldine edition of the *Comedia*: *Le terze rime di Dante* (1502). Oxford, Bodleian Library, Auct. 2R 7.12.

(Vatican Latin 3199). Bembo restored Dante to a more authentic linguistic setting, but his edition also signalled a notable downgrading of Dante's status, since it contained no commentary and used a title, *Le terze rime di Dante* ('The Tercets of Dante'), that relegated the *Commedia* to the genre of vernacular verse. Bembo's edition marked the beginning of a formalist treatment of Dante and his marginalization in relation to the vernacular works of Petrarch and Boccaccio (Fig. 38). Bembo's own later proposals for reform of the Italian language found fullest expression in his *Prose della volgar lingua* ('Prose on the Vernacular Language', 1525), where he not only established Petrarch and Boccaccio as vernacular models for poetry and prose, but openly criticized Dante for his indiscriminate use of subject-matter, for licentiousness, and for unharmoniously mixing Latin, foreign, non-Tuscan, dated, and rough words. For Bembo the result was that the *Commedia* could 'justifiably be compared to a beautiful spacious field of wheat which is interspersed all over with oats, tares, and sterile, harmful grasses'.[66]

The Venetian Bembo may have helped to establish the Trecento Florentine vernacular as the literary language of the peninsula, but, at the same time, he served to marginalize both Dante and Florentine culture of the Cinquecento. Inevitably, Florentines such as Girolamo Benivieni (1453–1542) – who, in 1506, produced one of only two Florentine editions of the poem in the sixteenth century – leapt to the poet's defence. However, in a century where Venetian initiatives and Bembist paradigms tended to dominate, the most important Florentine reassertion of Dante came with the public readings and related publications of the state-sponsored Florentine Academy. This Academy, established on 11 February 1541 by Duke Cosimo I (1537–74), stood at the heart of Florentine cultural life, regulating scholarly and literary activities, including printing.

In the Florentine Academy the readings or *lezioni* of Dante from the 1540s to the 1580s offered a vision of the *Commedia* as a *summa* of doctrinal knowledge and presented an implicit reply to Bembo's reservations regarding the poem's content. The *lezioni* were public, unlike those on Petrarch, and often served as a pretext for the promotion and classicization of the vernacular, for handling controversial issues of contemporary theology and philosophy, and for engaging in the debate on which dialect was best suited for Italy – a debate complicated by the rediscovery of Dante's own *De vulgari eloquentia* ('On Vernacular Eloquence', 1304–6), which, with its advocacy of an illustrious Italian vernacular, was used to counter the claims made for the pre-eminent status of Florentine.[67]

One of the first to lecture on Dante was Pierfrancesco Giambullari (1495–1555), author of various academic lessons and an unfinished commentary on the *Inferno*, who gives an enthusiastic estimate of Dante's manifold competence in theology, astrology, and cosmography. Similar emphases are found in Cosimo Bartoli (1503–72), advisor to Giorgio

Vasari (1511–74) and vernacular translator of Alberti and Ficino, who gave seven lectures dealing with the eye, faith, happiness, eternity, the creation of the world, and the power of God. In his second lecture, Bartoli made unorthodox use of the controversial reformist text, the *Beneficio di Cristo* ('The Kindness of Christ').

Of particular interest and complexity is Giovanni Battista Gelli (1498–1563), a Florentine shoemaker, who became official commentator on Dante at the Academy from 1553 until his death in 1563. Gelli's readings show a close concern to elucidate Dante's text (his detailed linguistic observations are often directed at praising Florentine), as well as a keen interest in moralizing and philosophical reading. Like Bartoli, there are traces of reformist interest; and, like other readers in the Academy,[68] he interprets Dante through his minor works and with close reference to the earlier commentary tradition.

The most important academician of all, however, is the humanist Benedetto Varchi (1503 – 65). Varchi managed to reconcile some of Bembo's intuitions with praise of Dante, by preparing Florentine editions of the Venetian's works. He also drew upon his own studies of Aristotle at Padua in emphasizing Dante's philosophical learning, and sponsored the gathering of manuscripts in order to establish a more authoritative text. While efforts at greater linguistic appreciation of the *Commedia* were to bear most fruit outside of the Academy proper in Vincenzio Borghini (1515–80) and the severe grammatical and linguistic analyses of the Modenese Lodovico Castelvetro (1504/5 – 71), the philological ferment promoted by its members did lead to a Florentine edition of the *Commedia* (1595), sponsored by the newly formed Accademia della Crusca, that was based on an unprecedented number of collated manuscripts and attempted to supersede Bembo's text.

Even outside Florence, not all writers, humanists, and teachers shared Bembo's strictures against Dante. The Venetian *letterato* and teacher, Trifon Gabriele (1470–1549), in his lessons for aspiring writers, offered a more favourable judgment, emphasizing Dante's excellence in the use of metaphor and simile. A tone of decidedly anti-Bembo polemic infiltrates the Venetian edition of the *Commedia* published by Francesco Marcolini da Forlì in 1544 with commentary by the Lucchese Alessandro Vellutello (Fig. 39). Vellutello's 'Dante', complete with an important set of illustrations, went through four abbreviated editions (Roville in Lyons: 1551, 1552, 1571, and 1575), and the three reprintings by Sansovino mentioned earlier, where Vellutello's commentary appeared alongside Landino's glosses. Striking a polemical note in his 'Letter to the Readers', Vellutello charges Bembo's Aldine editions with textual corruption. Compared with Landino, Vellutello's commentary is notable for the closer attention it pays to literal textual commentary and the reduced number of digressions. Vellutello also makes much of reading Dante with Dante (especially the *Convivio* ('Banquet', 1303–06/07), the most reprinted of his minor works, starting with a first Florentine edition in

1490, and three Venetian editions in 1521 (Fig. 40), 1529 and 1531), and he is innovative in making detailed use, as an historical source, of the Trecento Florentine chronicler Giovanni Villani (*c.* 1275–1348).

In the second half of the Cinquecento, as the ascendancy of Petrarch becomes ever more pronounced, Dante continues to be printed and there are some ten Venetian editions between 1564 and 1578. Such printings coincide with a more pronounced interest in moral and religious matters in Counter-Reformation Italy. Yet some of Dante's other works fall foul of the new religious and moral orthodoxies: the inquisitorial censors of the 1576 edition of the *Vita nova* ('New Life', 1292–94) called for excisions of some religious vocabulary used to celebrate Beatrice; and the *Monarchia* (first printed in Basel by Giovanni Oporino in 1559) is listed in the *Index Librorum Prohibitorum* of 1564 (it was only removed in 1881). In this changed religious and political climate, the final three decades of the Cinquecento also see a new literary contestation of the *Commedia* in which Aristotle's *Poetics* provides the main point of reference. The *querelle* over Dante, ostensibly occasioned by a

39.
First page and first woodcut in Alessandro Vellutello, *La comedia di Dante Aligieri con la nova espositione di Alessandro Vellutello* (Venice: Francesco Marcolini, 1544). Oxford, Bodleian Library, Toynbee 3563.

40.
Portrait of Dante on title-
page in *Lo amoroso Convivio
di Dante* (Venice: Zuane
Antonio & Fratelli da Sabio,
1521). Oxford, Bodleian
Library, Toynbee 2875.

remark concerning Dante's superiority to Homer in Varchi's posthumous
Hercolano (1570), is started off by the still unidentified Ridolfo Castravilla
with his *Discorso nel quale si mostra l'imperfettione della Comedia di Dante* ('Discourse
in which the Imperfection of Dante's Comedy Is Revealed', 1572). Organized
entirely around a rigid understanding of the *Poetics*, the *Discorso* found the
Commedia wanting, particularly given its title, in its general status as a poem
and in particular features pertaining to plot, character, thought, and diction.
This attack elicited both supporters and antagonists in a climate of heated
yet highly artificial polemic. Of particular note are the defences of Dante
(1572 and 1573) by Jacopo Mazzoni (1548–98) and attempts to support
Castravilla against Mazzoni, such as that (1576) by Bellisario Bulgarini
(1538/39–*c.* 1621).

   The debate over Dante continued, at least in Italian Academies, into the
seventeenth century, but it remained narrow in direction and authoritarian
in scope. Perhaps unsurprisingly, given the climate of literary neo-classicism
that prevailed in the Seicento, the reputation of the *Commedia* now enters a
period of decline. Only a handful of editions are published in the Seicento,
and Landino's *Comento* is not supplanted until Pompeo Venturo's commentary
in 1732. It is not until the nineteenth century that the *Commedia* will re-emerge
from the margins to regain canonical status and elicit a range of responses –
critical and ideological, artistic and literary, erudite and popularizing – which,
in richness and complexity, is comparable to the ones charted in this chapter.

CHAPTER 5

Dante's nineteenth-century reception: Francesca da Rimini and the idea of Italy

Alex MacMillan

Where does one begin to elaborate Dante Alighieri's importance in the nineteenth century? He is everywhere we look: in the music of Piotr Tchaikovsky (1840–93), the paintings of the Pre-Raphaelites, the art criticism of John Ruskin (1819–1900), and he even makes an appearance in the political analysis of Karl Marx (1796–1877). Dante's cultural afterlife is so substantial that scholars have coined a noun and an adjective to refer to it: respectively, Dantism and Dantesque. The sheer volume of Dantesque allusions is unwieldy, yet if we try to limit our research, say to Dante in English, then we fail to register the enormity and the thoroughly international character of Dante-idolatry since the nineteenth century. Paget Toynbee, in his magisterial study of English Dantism, explores in the region of two hundred significant Dante citations in England, in the early nineteenth century alone.[69] But counting the numbers of citations of Dante also somehow misses the point, as T. S. Eliot (1888–1965) claimed when writing about his own relationship to Dante: 'the important debt ... does not occur in relation to the number of places in one's writings to which a critic can point a finger, and say, here and there he wrote something which could not have been written unless he had Dante in mind.'[70] How should one make sense of it all?

Dante's literary significance in the nineteenth century was far from one-dimensional; the century's Dantism was marked by a double movement. There was a degree of indifference to or even ignorance of the theological allegory that Dante employs; at the same time, the reception of Dante's work was conditioned by a very modern sort of allegory – the politics of the aesthetic sphere. Two dates serve as useful beacons for our history. The first is politically significant, and ostensibly unrelated to Dante's reception: the 1830 July Revolution in France, in which Louis Philippe, duc d'Orléans (1773–1850), replaced the Bourbon incumbent, Charles X (1757–1836). With France the political and intellectual hub of Europe, years of upheaval in

Paris had sent shockwaves throughout the rest of the continent. Yet the deposition of the Bourbons in 1830 was a manifest disappointment to republicans and liberal idealists alike. Thus Marie-Henri Beyle (1783–1842), better known as Stendhal, added to his bitterly ironic novel *Le Rouge et le Noir* ('The Red and the Black') the subtitle *Chronique de 1830*. In his mind the date had become synonymous with political disappointment: history had betrayed poets' idealism – perhaps words themselves had given false hope and made hypocrites of 'the unacknowledged legislators of the world'.[71]

Romantic disappointment with the monarchical revolution was compounded with the earlier fall of Napoleon in 1815. Although Napoleon Bonaparte (1769–1821) had been hated as much as he was loved, he had embodied the idea that one could realize the most fantastical dreams of success by will alone. French critic Paul Bénichou has argued that after 1830, poetry saw men of letters reject the public sphere and disengage from political action; political disillusion led to the creation of an autonomous aesthetic sphere, an 'école du désenchantement'.[72] The disenchantment of 1830 therefore served to uncouple poetry from overt political intent. It marked the end of continental Romanticism in its most vigorous phase, since words and high ideals could no longer convincingly claim to be agents of historical change. Dantism before 1830, therefore, bore a distinctly political character.

The second date, 1865, is significant since it marks the simultaneous claim of the Italian nation and of academe to control the interpretation of Dante's text. The year saw the first meeting of the Italian parliament in Florence and simultaneously the organized celebrations of Dante's sixth centenary. The cult of Dante thereby became inextricably linked with the Risorgimento. Henry Wadsworth Longfellow (1807–82), at the time America's most popular poet, sent his verse translation of the *Inferno* to Florence for the occasion (Fig. 41); by this offering Longfellow forged an important link between Italian and American Dantism. Florence's celebrations anticipated the formalization of American Dante studies with the founding of the Dante Society of America in Cambridge, Massachusetts, in 1881 under Longfellow's aegis. Longfellow's translation is marked by a sensitivity to the precise wording and syntax of the original Italian. Several years later, the principles of philology would be fully applied to Dante's text in the 1893 commentary to the *Commedia* by Giovanni Andrea Scartazzini (1837–1901) and in the edition of *De vulgari eloquentia* prepared by Pio Rajna (1847–1930), published the same year: these texts constitute early landmarks in Dante scholarship. Scartazzini's commentary, for example, provided an easy-to-use digest of the different ways in which individual words and short passages of the *Commedia* had been interpreted by the commentators since Dante's time. Together Scartazzini and Rajna signal the beginning of professional Dante scholarship as a discipline in its own right.

Dante's significance evolved quickly over the course of the century, but certain traits in popular Dantism remained constant. Chief among these was a vein of what we would now see as sentimentality. The Dantesque play by Silvio Pellico (1789–1854), *Francesca da Rimini*, which premiered in Milan in 1818, showcases this sentimental Dante. In the following passage the doomed lovers from the fifth canto of *Inferno*, Francesca and Paolo, confess the strength of their love:

> PAOLO   I will love you until my dying hour! ... even
> If for that profane love I must endure
> Hell's chastisement for all time
> I will love you still the same.
>
> FRANCESCA   Can it be?
> You will love me even there?[73]

The sentiments expressed, and the language in which they are framed, strike us as being purely conventional. The gushing passage gives a good idea of the play as a whole. The piece lacks any sophisticated engagement with Dante's poetry: it ignores the theological significance of Paolo and Francesca's self-centred, animalistic love. But perhaps the fact that today we would expect a degree of sophistication in a play inspired by Dante suggests how much attitudes to the poet have changed. Pellico's play puzzles and amuses us because it seems to try and make Dante into an opera librettist.

41.
On the left-hand page a sonnet by Longfellow; on the right-hand page his translation of the beginning of the *Inferno* (London, 1867). Oxford, Bodleian Library, Toynbee 2051, pp. 1–2.

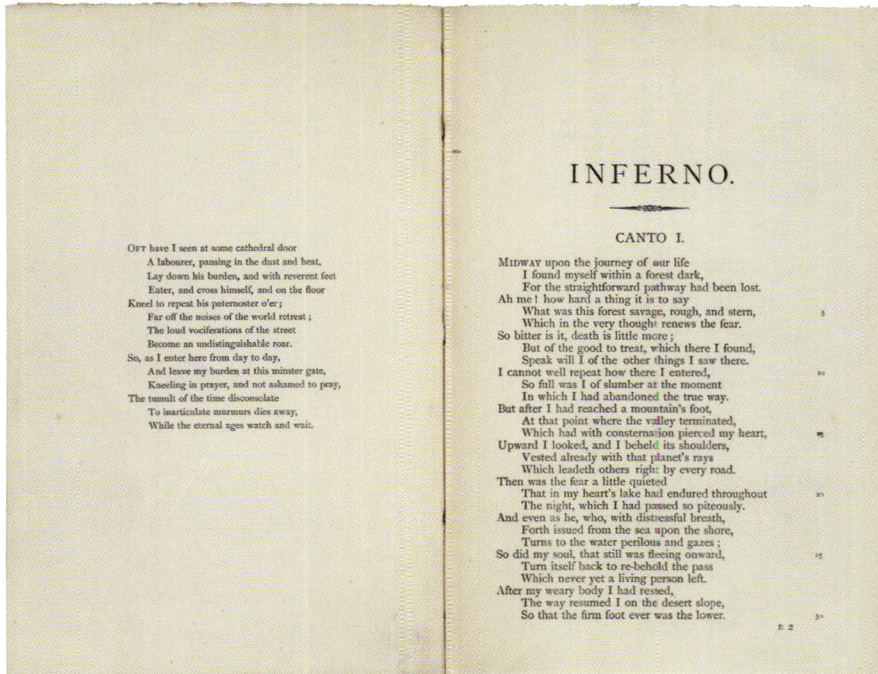

OFT have I seen at some cathedral door
A labourer, passing in the dust and heat,
Lay down his burden, and with reverent feet
Enter, and cross himself, and on the floor
Kneel to repeat his paternoster o'er ;
Far off the noises of the world retreat ;
The loud vociferations of the street
Become an undistinguishable roar.
So, as I enter here from day to day,
And leave my burden at this minster gate,
Kneeling in prayer, and not ashamed to pray,
The tumult of the time disconsolate
To inarticulate murmurs dies away,
While the eternal ages watch and wait.

INFERNO.

CANTO I.

MIDWAY upon the journey of our life
    I found myself within a forest dark,
    For the straightforward pathway had been lost.
Ah me ! how hard a thing it is to say
    What was this forest savage, rough, and stern,
    Which in the very thought renews the fear.
So bitter is it, death is little more ;
    But of the good to treat, which there I found,
    Speak will I of the other things I saw there.
I cannot well repeat how there I entered,
    So full was I of slumber at the moment
    In which I had abandoned the true way.
But after I had reached a mountain's foot,
    At that point where the valley terminated,
    Which had with consternation pierced my heart,
Upward I looked, and I beheld its shoulders,
    Vested already with that planet's rays
    Which leadeth others right by every road.
Then was the fear a little quieted
    That in my heart's lake had endured throughout
    The night, which I had passed so piteously.
And even as he, who, with distressful breath,
    Forth issued from the sea upon the shore,
    Turns to the water perilous and gazes ;
So did my soul, that still was fleeing onward,
    Turn itself back to re-behold the pass
    Which never yet a living person left.
After my weary body I had rested,
    The way resumed I on the desert slope,
    So that the firm foot ever was the lower.

Pellico's interpretation is, however, quite typical of much of the Dantism we encounter throughout the century. Hence scholars who have examined the poet's nineteenth-century reception complain that its Dantism is clichéd, sentimental, and run through with anachronistic misreadings of the original poem. There is a conventional rhetoric: the same allusions and the same critical commonplaces recur *ad nauseam*. Writing about early nineteenth-century English Dantism, one critic laments the Romantics' myopia: 'it soon became clear that, in spite of their professed enthusiasm, [the Romantics'] interest in the *Divina Commedia* was in most cases strictly limited to a few passages, almost exclusively from the *Inferno*.'[74] In assessing French enthusiasm for Dante, another scholar is more explicit in his disapproval, stating that the phenomenon was characterized by 'a purely superficial appreciation of the nature of [Dante's] art'; he concludes that the period's critical and artistic responses were the result of a lethal concoction of enthusiasm and ignorance.[75] Let us consider some of the instances of this enthusiasm and ignorance.

Silvio Pellico was certainly not alone in isolating Francesca da Rimini for extended treatment: no other of Dante's creations had proved as popular during the century.[76] Francesca da Rimini (1255–85), who makes an appearance in the fifth canto of the *Inferno*, is a real historical figure, and for Dante she belonged to recent history. She was an adulteress slain by her husband Gianciotto after he discovered her amorous involvement with his own brother, Paolo. In the nineteenth century Francesca rapidly became a *cause célèbre* whose fame inspired work across the arts. Notable among those artists who painted her were Jean Auguste Dominique Ingres (1780–1864), William Blake (1757–1827), and Gustave Doré (1832–83). The Paolo and Francesca scene was also one of the scenes from the *Commedia* which Auguste Rodin (1840–1917) began to sculpt after he received a commission in 1880 for a bronze gate for the Musée des Arts Décoratifs, Paris. Numerous Italian artists attempted Francesca-related subjects: by mid-century this pictorial tradition had informed the composition of other, strictly unrelated, themes, as in the 1851 oil painting by Costantino Sereno (1829–93), *Niccolò de' Lapi sorprende Lamberto che dà il primo bacio d'amore a Laudomia* ('Niccolò dei Lapi Surprises Lamberto Kissing Laudomia for the First Time') – in Sereno's painting Niccolò de' Lapi appears in the role of Francesca's cuckolded husband Gianciotto. For the 1865 Dante exhibition in Florence, Pietro Benvenuti (1769–1844) had his *Dante incontra Paolo e Francesca da Rimini* ('Dante Meets Paolo and Francesca da Rimini') shown, which was notable for restoring Dante as a witness to the dramatic scene. Francesca also held a fascination for the Pre-Raphaelite Brotherhood, as part of an obsessive interest in the figure of Dante as a lover who sublimated his desire: Dante Gabriel Rossetti (1828–82) depicted the subject twice in 1855 and once more in 1862.[77]

But let us return to Silvio Pellico's earlier work, which belongs to pre-1830 Dantism. It is important to bear in mind that Pellico was an Italian patriot who was imprisoned by the Austrians in 1820 for his involvement with the Carbonari. With this background information, we can see how in Pellico's text, Paolo's romantic ardour is an indirect expression of the author's underlying political passion. Here Paolo speaks as though he were one of Napoleon's war veterans returning from campaign:

> PAOLO   Worn out by glory's visions, I return.
> My blood has flowed, Byzantium, for you.
> I've fought for you without hate in my veins.
> The emperor, benevolent, rained honours
> Upon my head. But the general acclaim
> Now sickens more than it excites my heart.
> My sword is spattered from pointless slaughter,
> For foreign lands — and have I not my own,
> To whom our people are bound by bloodline?
> For you, for you, land of an ennobled race,
> My Italy, I will contend. The fiend
> Who rapes you now shall not escape unhurt.
> Fairest of lands, on you the Sun shines still.[78]

The Italian émigré Antonio Gallergo (1810–95) recalled the play's immense popularity in Milan. While attending a performance he had admired its 'wild enthusiasm and transport, all that vague mixture of ardent and delicate feelings'. Of this passage he observes that 'it never fails to be received with a thundering applause by an Italian audience'.[79] The belligerent language seems out of place in a play ostensibly given over to passions of another variety: what are we to make of this curious admixture of ardent and delicate feeling? A brief discussion of what informed contemporary attitudes towards delicate feelings should help to explain the strident tone of Pellico's work.

While in modern usage the term 'sentimental' is pejorative, implying superficiality or a redundancy of feeling, the nineteenth century was inheritor to an Enlightenment valorization of the term. Adam Smith (1723–90), in his *Theory of Moral Sentiments* (1759), made it clear that he considered moral propriety to be premised on sentiment — that is, on emotional, imaginative identification. If our brother is on the rack, he noted, then although physically we feel nothing, yet we are moved by the impressions of our senses: 'By the imagination we place ourselves in his situation, we conceive ourselves enduring all the same torments, we enter, as it were, into his body'[80]. Not only is 'fellow-feeling' a prerequisite for moral action, but the extent to which we possess it acts as an index of the liveliness of our intelligence.

Influential though this theory was, by the late eighteenth century it had begun to come under attack; pure sentiment was no longer seen as inherently desirable. The English in particular were warned off sentiment by the excesses of the French Revolution. Edmund Burke (1729–97) said categorically that, owing to the malign influence of Jean-Jacques Rousseau (1712–78), a new public morality had been instilled in the leaders of France's National Assembly, one whose object, 'is to merge all natural and social sentiment in inordinate vanity', and whose character, in Burke's damning phrase, is to show 'Benevolence to the whole species, and want of feeling for every individual.'[81] Thus the protagonists in the novels of Jane Austen (1775–1817), like Elinor Dashwood in *Sense and Sensibility* (1811), act as vehicles for the sage advice that there is no safe sensibility unless it is held in check by good sense. How, then, do we account for the growing ardour and the depths of feeling aroused by the thought of Francesca and, to an extent, at the very mention of Dante?

For Burke and Austen, sensibility came to be identified with anti-sociability – it was seen as being an essentially solipsistic experience.[82] But it seems clear, from the clichéd return to certain critical *lieux par excellence* in Dante's poem, that nineteenth-century readers of Dante were highly sociable. In *Nightmare Abbey* (1818), a playful parody of Romantic literary culture by Thomas Love Peacock (1785–1866), Mr Listless realizes he needs a copy of Dante in order to be accepted at social gatherings. He remarks, 'I find [Dante] is growing fashionable, and I am afraid I must read him some wet morning' (Fig. 42).[83] Fashion may be superficial; it is never solipsistic. And in this case, even the seeming superficiality of that fashion is quite deceptive. Silvio Pellico's success as a popular playwright suggests that what we see in Romantic Dantism is nothing less than a successful redefinition and rehabilitation of sentiment. Fellow-feeling is dissociated from the excesses that had disgraced the French Revolution and instead is conjoined to the Italian nationalist cause. In the first flush of Italian Romanticism, Francesca became a metaphor for Italy: in Pellico's words, 'For you, for you, land of an ennobled race, / My Italy, I will contend'. Therefore, when Francesca's nineteenth-century admirers insistently stressed their compassion for her, they also referred indirectly to their credentials as sensitive and politically *bien-pensant* readers. Francesca served as a shibboleth, a cornerstone of the new bourgeois, aesthetic sociability, and of the new middle-class's international political conscience.

This political interpretation should help explain why nineteenth-century critics and artists vied with one another to declare their compassion. None could find superlatives sufficiently strong to communicate the strength of his feelings. John Keats (1795–1821) recalls in a letter to George and Georgiana Keats in 1819 that 'the fifth canto of Dante pleases me more and more'; his constantly accruing delight in the passage outstrips any single articulation. Definitive proof of an authentic experience of the poetry

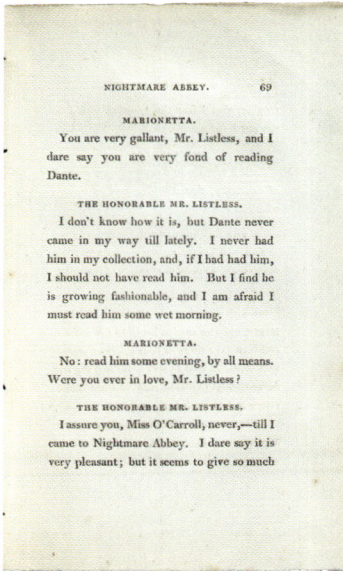

42.
Peacock's parodic dialogue
shows the popularity of
Dante around 1818. Thomas
Love Peacock, *Nightmare
Abbey* (London, 1818).
Oxford, Bodleian Library, 12
θ 552, p. 69.

was having a vision of one's own. For Keats, in 1819, reading of Dante's encounter with Francesca caused him to dream. He describes how in the dream he 'floated upon the whirling atmosphere as it is described with a beautiful figure to whose lips mine were joined as it seemed for an age'.[84] When he wakes he composes a sonnet, 'As Hermes Once Took to his Feathers Light'. In 1826 William Hazlitt (1778–1830) reports a similar flight of literary fancy, although his object is this time not Francesca but Pia de' Tolomei, from the fifth canto of the *Purgatorio*: 'O Siena! If I felt charmed with thy narrow, tenantless streets, or looked delighted through thy arched gateway over the subjected plain, it was that some recollections of Madonna Pia hung upon the beatings of my spirit, and converted a barren waste into the regions of romance!'[85]

From the substance of Hazlitt's vision, it might as well have been Francesca as Pia whom he recalled; the sentiments are the same, and so too is the fanciful translation of the landscape into one proper to a medieval romance. The dreamer envisages having a direct, personal encounter with the heroine. Comparing Keats and Hazlitt, the sentiment and core elements are strikingly familiar – yet Keats's comments are part of a private letter. The echo, therefore, indicates not direct influence, but the extent of the consensus about Dante's merits in a newly transformed and politically charged public sphere. The real beauty of pre-1830s Dantism lies in its subtle dissidence. It was subversive not in its content (for it would be an oversimplification to claim all Romantic Dantists belonged to the same political camp) but in its choice of subject and in its style. Pellico's *Francesca da Rimini*, with a subject apparently safely distanced in history, slipped past the Austrian censors to premiere in Milan. Keats's letter uses Dante to

mediate between the private, contemplative sphere and the realm of shared
sentiment (a precursor to action, in Adam Smith's view). Finally, Hazlitt's
prose style, in its blend of the literary and the conversational registers (his
'plain speaking' manner), is perhaps the stylistic analogue of a democratized,
people's Dante – literary criticism presented in the form of travelogue.[86]
From the point of view of the authorities, such private aesthetic networking
is far more insidious than the circulation of political pamphlets.

By the middle of the century, Italian patriots no longer needed such
delicacy of political statement. The greatest Italian critic of the age,
Francesco De Sanctis (1817–83), expressed the same admiration for Dante
as had his predecessors, but the tone of his criticism is more one of the
triumphant literary anthologist. De Sanctis's praise for Dante was part of his
grander ambition to create awareness of an authentic and unbroken Italian
national literature. He, too, writes of the Francesca passage: 'You cannot
resist a sense of heartbreak as you see them draw, smiling and carefree,
closer and closer to the abyss they are digging for themselves, in which all
their youth and beauty will be engulfed almost before they taste the joys of
life.'[87] Potent sentiment has been translated into nostalgia in De Sanctis's
analysis. In 1861 De Sanctis had been politically dignified by his appointment
as Minister for Public Instruction under unified Italy's first Prime Minister,
Camillo Benso di Cavour (1810–61); he therefore had no need to make veiled
reference to his political aspirations. Yet, although the political tension
has gone, De Sanctis's Francesca never ceases to be a symbol of Italy.
Revolutionary France had Marianne; for De Sanctis, Italy has Francesca.
Francesca is neither virgin nor whore – she possesses a metonymic power:
'even if guilty, we feel [she is] part of ourselves, of our common nature'.[88]
After De Sanctis, instances of popular Dantism seem to elide politics
altogether. The music of the late Romantic period is an excellent illustration
of this.

In 1876 Tchaikovsky wrote a symphonic fantasy for Francesca, the
Fantaisie d'après Dante, op. 32, and he was followed by Rachmaninov (1873–
1943), who wrote an opera for her in 1906. For Tchaikovsky the poetry is
love lyric, pure and simple: 'I wrote it with love, and that love, it seems,
has come out quite well.' The piece was not based on Dante directly, but
on the etching by Gustave Doré. Tchaikovsky comments modestly, 'As for
the whirlwind, something might have been written to better correspond to
Doré's illustration.'[89] The allusion to Doré is telling, for like the successful
illustrator's work, there is a highly pictorial, decorative tendency to Dantism
after unification. De Sanctis's popular *Storia della letteratura italiana* ('History
of Italian Literature', 1870) seeks to make a continuous narrative, to
mythologize and so embellish Italian history. Doré and Tchaikovsky, in a
similar vein, attend to successful mimetic techniques. Gabriele D'Annunzio
(1863–1938) returned to the subject in the form of a play. His *Francesca da*

Rimini (1901) is aestheticized to the point where it became an exquisite artefact.[90] D'Annunzio's *Francesca* played in Rome on 9 December 1901; his lover, the ravishing Eleanora Duse, played Francesca. The 1902 Italian edition of the text is fully illustrated, an *objet d'art*, and its decoration and preparation were overseen personally by the author.[91] Arthur Symons, D'Annunzio's English translator, compares the piece with Wagnerian opera, similar 'in his over-amplification of detail, his insistence on so many things beside the essential things, his recapitulations, into which he has brought almost the actual Wagnerian "motives"'.[92] Sure enough, the play was converted into a libretto for an opera with music by Riccardo Zandonai (1883–1944). The reader-response that late-nineteenth century Dantism seeks to elicit is sympathy stripped of the possibility of action. It becomes instead intensely voyeuristic. Matching the decline in politicized Dantism, Paolo lost his virility over the years (the same might be said for poetry as an expressive form). Paolo remains silent in Dante's poem as Francesca tells their tale. He was quickly recast, therefore, as the effete aesthete. In Gilbert and Sullivan's 1881 comic opera, *Patience*, he is invoked to mock the Paterian aesthete, a 'Francesca da Rimini, nimminy-piminny young man'.[93]

After D'Annunzio, the twentieth-century's fascination with Dante was of a very different order. In the anglophone world T. S. Eliot did most to ensure this. Eliot's use of Dante in *The Waste Land* (1922) reversed the nineteenth century's vulgarized and sentimental fascination with certain passages in the *Commedia*. In Eliot's hands Dante's poetry became arcane. Eliot achieved this in two ways: he avoided quoting from any of the passages that had been popular in the previous century, and he inserted in his poetry passages from Dante which he left untranslated, even though the nineteenth century had been replete with good English translations. (The best full English version in the Romantic period had been the one published in 1814 as *The Vision*, by Reverend Henry Francis Cary; much more accurate was Henry Wadsworth Longfellow's full translation of 1867.) Eliot seemingly overlooked this tradition. His interest in Dante, therefore, owes an important debt to the Dante cults of the nineteenth century, but as a reaction against them. His interpretation is a radical departure from the spirit of his predecessors' Dantism. Perhaps this departure was necessary: he cut away much of the fat that had gathered around Dante's bones over the course of a century's fanaticism. But in doing so he failed to do justice to a tradition which had obsessively revisited the same moments in Dante's poem, and which had unfailingly found new things to admire on each occasion.

CHAPTER 6

Dante and the *Rossetti* family

John Woodhouse

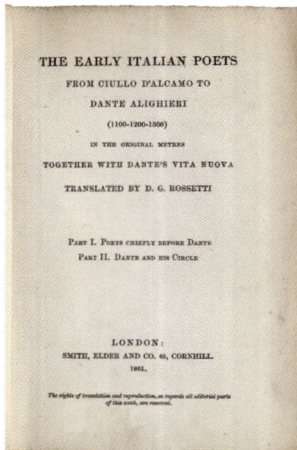

THE EARLY ITALIAN POETS

FROM CIULLO D'ALCAMO TO

DANTE ALIGHIERI

(1100-1200-1300)

IN THE ORIGINAL METRES

TOGETHER WITH DANTE'S VITA NUOVA

TRANSLATED BY D. G. ROSSETTI

PART I. POETS CHIEFLY BEFORE DANTE
PART II. DANTE AND HIS CIRCLE

LONDON:
SMITH, ELDER AND CO. 65, CORNHILL.
1861.

*The rights of translation and reproduction, as regards all editorial parts
of this work, are reserved.*

43.
Rossetti's fine translation of
Dante's youthful work, the
Vita Nova, in Dante Gabriel
Rossetti, *The Early Italian
Poets, in the Original Metres.
Together with Dante's Vita Nuova*
(London, 1861). Oxford,
Bodleian Library, Toynbee
2310, title-page.

The life and work of Dante Alighieri found many resonances in the small but powerful cultural dynasty founded in London after 1826 by Gabriele Rossetti (1783–1854). None of the Rossetti family went untouched by the influence of Dante. Gabriele's eldest child, Maria Francesca, published an edition of the *Divine Comedy* in English (1871) which, owing to its straightforward, popular approach and lack of complex theorizing, outsold her father's commentary on the *Inferno*. Her younger brother, William Michael, did much unseen or unacknowledged work on Dante, including the translation of the prose passages in Dante Gabriel's beautiful version of the *Vita nova* (1861) (Fig. 43).[94] He also published his own verse translation of the *Inferno* (1865), and later did a useful prose translation of *Convivio* (1910). The youngest child, Christina, remained an enthusiastic reader of Dante until the end of her life, and although she sporadically left interesting thoughts in letters and essays, she never became actively involved in any exegesis of his writings. Even Frances Polidori-Rossetti, whom Gabriele married in 1826, had a hand in her husband's work after his death, when — perhaps out of kindness — she destroyed the 2,500 unsold volumes of his explanatory study *Il mistero dell'amor platonico* (1840), which Gabriele's patrons had advised him to withdraw from sale a decade earlier.

It was Gabriele himself, however, and his more famous son Dante Gabriel, who were more obviously and more strongly influenced by their study of Dante. Both had a concept of close parallels between Dante's legacy and their own life and work which created fascinating literary and artistic cruces. The biographical similarities between his own life and Dante's conjured up critical theories which so obsessed old Gabriele that they brought him ridicule, despair, and failure, while for his less academically minded artist son (at least in his more happy-go-lucky youth) the parallels brought inspiration, fame, and fortune.

Gabriele Rossetti was already forty-one years old when he landed in Britain as a political exile in 1824. He did, however, have excellent references, and was convinced that if he were prepared to be energetic and punctilious there were good prospects for him in a London full of Italophiles. He had already enjoyed several careers in Italy, including his appointment (1807–20) as curator of antiquities at the renowned Archaeological Museum in Naples. He was author of a considerable corpus of published poetry, and rejoiced in an unrivalled reputation as an extempore poet (*improvvisatore*), his services being in particular demand as librettist at the Teatro San Carlo. In 1815 Napoleon's regent, General Murat (Re Gioacchino), had sent him to Rome as Secretary for Education and Fine Arts. And, by the time of Rossetti's exile from Naples, he had been elected associate of several of the more prestigious southern Italian academies, including the Arcadia and the Accademia Tiberina.[95]

Rossetti's comfortable situation in Naples was thrown into turmoil after the fall of Napoleon in 1815, the subsequent expulsion of Murat, and the Bourbons' return from Sicily to their capital city. By 1820 Rossetti had become a well-known agitator for constitutional reform, a top-ranking officer of the Carbonari, and secretary of their *Distretto napoletano*:

> And the Carbonari, the invincible sect,
> broadest assemblage of daring spirits,
> were spreading with irresistible force,
> like a vast forest fire fanned by the wind.[96]

Rossetti and his fellow conspirators were initially sanguine that the returning monarch, Ferdinand I, would accept the idea of a constitutional monarchy. But all their hopes were dashed when Ferdinand's forces, stiffened by his Austrian allies, defeated the constitutionalists at the battle of Antrodoco in March 1821.

Gabriele's immediate disappointment had given rise in 1820 to his *Odi civiche/Odi cittadine* ('Civic Odes'), exalting liberty and cursing tyranny, with dire references to the contemporary regime. The poems were received with wild enthusiasm in the city and marked him out as a dangerous element, to be taken dead or alive by Ferdinand's secret police.[97] In 1821, after dodging the *sbirri* for three months in the Concordia district of the city, and thanks to the good offices of Lady Moore, an admirer of his poetry, Rossetti was smuggled aboard the flagship of her husband, the English admiral Sir Graham Moore. Exiled briefly to Malta, Rossetti was to see Naples again only once, from the deck of Moore's vessel on his way to permanent exile in England.

On Malta he made several influential friends, including the Frere family.[98] John Hookham Frere undoubtedly helped persuade Rossetti to turn his mind to more serious academic matters and to a larger European stage, rather than relying on his improvisatory skills and Italian language classes, within the narrow limits of the island. Henry Cary's brilliant translation of the *Commedia* had already come out to great applause in 1814, and there was a growing fashion for Dante in London. What more natural than that Frere should discuss with his new protégé the possibility of his producing an edition of Dante's work? On Malta Rossetti learned the *Commedia* by heart (apparently no difficult task for an expert *improvvisatore*), and began to read all he could in Frere's and other libraries there. Later, on board the ship carrying him away from Frere and Malta, Rossetti composed a dream-like vision – *L'ombra di Dante* ('Dante's Shade') – in which he has an encounter with the shade of Dante, who is quick to compare their two destinies:[99]

> Both driven from our homes,
> both most wrongfully – who more than we?
> [...]. Both martyrs to love of our country.

And in the poem, Dante entrusts to Rossetti the mission to illuminate the secrets of his *Commedia*:

> You will understand in my secret words
> that ineffable truth which you invoke so assiduously,
> that truth which, obscure to so many, is clear to a few.
> [...] An exile yourself, you will understand the heart of an exile.[100]

Recommended by his influential friends as a teacher to some of the wealthier bourgeois families in West London, Rossetti was soon earning half a guinea an hour for each private Italian lesson. His first written mention of Dante studies was noted in 1824, during an exchange of letters with Lady Moore and with Susan Frere, daughter of the ambassador, while an earlier London letter shows that an enthusiastic student paid him three pounds for lessons on the *Commedia* in July of the same year.[101] Correspondence with a cautious Henry Cary was at least not explicitly discouraging. Rossetti had lent Cary part of the manuscript of his forthcoming *Comento analitico* ('Analytical Commentary') on Dante's *Inferno*, and Cary asked him to include his name among the subscribers, should he publish it by subscription.[102] By 1825 the first volume of the *Comento* was ready for publication. Rossetti's preparation had been impeccable. He had read all the commentaries available to him, and had discussed the current situation with several dilettante Dantists in London. He had also read every book on freemasonry that he could obtain.

Here lay the rub. Unfortunately for Gabriele, all his academic work was rendered useless by the absurdity of the underlying thesis: that Dante,

like Rossetti, had been oppressed by tyranny, like Rossetti had been driven
into exile, like Rossetti must have been part of a sect, in effect a secret
society, which closed ranks to protect its members against church and state
oppression, and used cryptography to communicate. Rossetti's Carbonari
used secret passwords and cyphers to safeguard their membership and mask
their activities. Dante's code was expressed through intricate variations on
the allegorical method which distinguished all his compositions. Poetry,
political oppression, exile, corruption in the Roman church, and a mania
for conspiracy theory and masonic lore all helped create in Rossetti
obsessions which tormented him for the following quarter of a century. In
particular Rossetti considered that certain of his own insights into Dante
revealed biographical coincidences which enhanced his understanding
and appreciation, not only of the *Commedia*, but also of the *Vita nova*, the
early poetry, *Monarchia*, and *Convivio*. Gabriele traced these ideas to his own
masonic experiences, but they clearly depended also upon intuitive, illusory
'insights', born of his traumatic experiences in Naples and bordering on
psychosis and persecution mania.

In spite of his cabalistic delusions, Rossetti's approach to the *Commedia*
would later become the traditional method of attempting to explain
Dante's representations of historical events in allegorical form. Some of
his explanations were undoubtedly informative for general readers and
enthusiasts, such as Charles Lyell, and even for less favourable critics such as
James Blunt, who found interest in the interpretation, but was not convinced
by 'the theory'.[103] Rossetti's approach was to illuminate and inspire later
commentators, too – among them Giovanni Pascoli (1855–1912) – who forced
themselves to disregard Rossetti's masonic notions. Rossetti was particularly
good at assimilating traditional philological interpretations of the *Commedia*,
examining and discussing ancient and modern commentators, checking and
comparing readings of different codices, lexical forms, critical opinions. His
knowledge of linguistic nuances, for instance, enabled him to explain why
the language surrounding the Farinata episode was recognizably more Tuscan
than elsewhere. He ignored the Romantic interpretation of episodes such as
that of Paolo and Francesca to reveal the sordid and tragic historical reality
of the episode. By contrast Ugo Foscolo (1778–1827) contemporaneously
suggested in his *Discorso sul testo della Divina Commedia* ('Discourse on the Text
of the *Divine Comedy*', 1825) that their sin was 'redeemed by the ardour of their
passion': 'in all those verses, compassion seems the only Muse'.[104]

Rossetti's allegorical interpretation of the three beasts of *Inferno* I
encapsulates many of these elements. He explains the beasts in terms of
Dante's personal experiences: opposed by the *Lonza* (Leopard) of Florence,
exiled because of the political influence of the French *Leone* (Lion), and
constantly persecuted by the papacy and the *Lupa* (She-wolf), identifiable
with avaricious Guelfism. He then connects *Lupa/Lupo/Wolf* with the origins

of the Guelf party. Considering the historical development of *Guelf* from Lothario Wolf, he notes that 'wolf' latinized produces *Guelfus*, and that in ancient Saxon, modern German, and living English, it means *Lupo*.[105] Connections between avarice, characteristic of the wolf and of the medieval papacy, the avaricious Judas in the mouth of Satan, and Pluto ('Cursed wolf', *Inf.* VII. 8) lead him to speculate on the meaning of the traditionally baffling opening line of *Inf.* VII – 'Papé Satàn, Papé Satàn Aleppe' – and to interpret it as implying that the realm of the avaricious is sacred to *Pope Satan, Pope Satan Prince*.[106] Rossetti's merits are at once visible in the text of the *Comento analitico*, and certainly interested his earliest readers. At the same time his cabalistic references to secret sects and to *fedeli d'amore* (Love's faithful servants) as adherents of those sects, baffled even his most sympathetic supporters.

His gravest error was to place too much emphasis on cabalistic ideas, the secret language (*gergo*) or jargon of sects, the notion of a primitive masonic anti-papal movement. He suggests that the language of all that Dante wrote was bound up in such cryptographic jargon and aimed at initiates; that Dante used secret language, allusive structures, even broken words and syllables, or locutions such as palindromes and anagrams. Rossetti was willing to spread his cryptographic theories very widely. His mania reached beyond Dante to include all the language of the Trecento which had, he thought, clear implications of a political and sectarian or masonic kind. In the political reality of his own era, in the struggles for Italian independence, and in the need for constitutional reform in Naples, he discerned part of a similar if contemporary problem, projecting the struggles of Guelf and Ghibelline on to the canvas of the Risorgimento. With a vast, imaginative but self-deluding leap, he applied those ingredients to resolving the allegory of Dante's great epic, as well as to interpreting the *Vita nova* and other medieval and Renaissance texts. He later extended his notions to much of Europe's great literature, including Milton's epics and Bunyan's *The Pilgrim's Progress*.[107]

Intelligent friends who declared themselves baffled by his theories sounded frequent warning notes to Rossetti. However, to add to the obsessiveness which bordered on fanaticism, Rossetti had character faults: against naive and over-polite supporters he stubbornly upheld his theories, and used straw victories to camouflage his own mortification. An innocent query by Frere or Lyell might be met with a defensive letter running to over a dozen pages of minute handwriting, every line begging new questions. His concepts provided easy targets for his detractors, notably for Antonio Panizzi (1797–1879), his rival for the chair at London's newly founded University College. Panizzi suggested that any reader feeling convinced by such theories needed his eyes opened by a surgeon's scalpel rather than by the opinions of a critic.[108] As late as the 1970s Mario Praz could not resist a dig at the desperate attempt to reveal a Dante written in lemon juice.[109]

In an effort to counter the indifference of critics and the hostility of others, and before completing his exegesis of the whole of the *Commedia*, Rossetti (who had been elected in 1831 to the new chair of Italian at King's College, London) set out to explain his main theses. This led to the publication of the study *Sullo spirito antipapale che produsse la riforma* ('On the Anti-Papal Spirit that Led to the Reformation', 1832), the five-volume edition of *Il mistero dell'Amor platonico dei medioevo derivato da' misteri antichi* ('The Mystery of Platonic Love in the Middle Ages, Derived from Ancient Mysteries', 1840), and *La Beatrice di Dante* ('Dante's Beatrice', 1842).[110] With these he hoped to clarify his ideas and present a more systematic version of his interpretations; but his analyses showed ever more preoccupation with jargon, sects, mysteries, and messianic implications. His *Comento analitico al Purgatorio* ('Analytical Commentary on the Purgatorio'), though completed possibly by 1830, was not published during his lifetime; its tattered ghost was edited only in 1966-67 by Pompeo Giannantonio.[111] The projected six-volume, full commentary on the *Commedia* was abandoned.

The *Spirito antipapale* was the first of his explanatory studies specifically concerned with his system. Its basis lay in the well-known spirit of opposition to the papacy among certain medieval Christians because of what they perceived as papal corruption. The violent reaction of the Church forced their opponents to be more cautious and less open – hence the creation for the initiates of a secret allegorical and anagogical language. Dante, one of those wanting to reform the Church and affirm the universal empire noted in the *Monarchia*, employed various cryptograms which could unite all opponents throughout Europe in what amounted to a secret society that Rossetti called the *setta d'amore* (Sect of Love), whose cryptic language pervaded medieval love poetry. Followers sighed for a *Donna* (*domina*) who represented their own political and religious ideals. In the *Vita nova*, and then the *Commedia*, Dante used that arcane language, symbolism and allegory.

Rossetti wrote the five-volume *Il mistero dell'amor platonico* to explain his theories systematically and historically. He traced his ideas back to the mysteries visible in the obscure rites and religious ceremonies of civilizations such as those of Egypt or Greece. From these ancient sects, he thought, descended such groups as Manicheans, Patarenes, Flagellants, Cathars, Lollards, Albigensians, Templars, and a host of others who maintained their own coded languages to protect themselves. More to his point, Rossetti thought that Provençal troubadors hid sectarian secrets in poems concerning love and ladies. The same was true of Italy and its first poets, notably at the Sicilian court of the Holy Roman Emperor, Frederick II. Frederick, the anti-papal Ghibelline, developed the erotic jargon, promoting a more refined mysticism that took the character of a purer love – Platonic love – which dominated medieval literature and had followers in Italy and abroad. Dante belonged to that secret sect. Centuries later, the masonic movement (which

44.
Lyell's translation of
Dante's lyric poems shows
the popularity even of
his minor works in the
nineteenth century. Charles
Lyell, *The Canzoniere of
Dante Alighieri Including the
Poems of the Vita Nuova and
Convito* (John Murray, 1842).
Oxford, Taylorian Library,
VET. ITAL. IV. B. 157, title
page.

included groups such as the *Carboneria*) was for Rossetti a logical derivation from these ancient organizations. He explains the evolving changes in the erotic jargon elaborated by Dante, from *Vita nova* and the lyric poetry to the *Commedia.*

Rossetti's *La Beatrice di Dante* had its first part or *ragionamento* published in 1842. With this work Rossetti proposed to close his twenty years of research into Dante. The major objective of his essay was to identify Beatrice, seen over the centuries as both a real and an imaginary figure. He assumes that the *Vita nova* and *Convivio* are two parts of one and the same work. The beatifying woman is a single individual identifiable with Philosophy, who appears in both sections, of which the first declares the problem or enigma and the second offers the solution to Dante's use of allegory. The *Vita nova* is the first stage in initiating readers into the hidden meanings of Dante's language, of which the *Commedia* is the supreme stage and the artistic culmination. The woman of the *Vita nova*, despite the illusory appearances, is the same creation as in *Convivio*, and represents Philosophy.

Rossetti was a graphomaniac, and after these distressing years, which had serious consequences for his health and the general well-being of his family, he devoted his time to less controversial volumes, many concerned with sacred songs and hymns (though he himself was no churchgoer). In these milder and uncontroversial spheres he found a ready market and popular esteem. But by 1850 the name Rossetti was becoming increasingly associated with his artistically talented son, Gabriel Charles Dante, whom he had named (as he proudly wrote to Charles Lyell) after his father, his godfather (Lyell), and Dante, in order to celebrate the great poet in the person of his first son.[112] Once out of his rebellious teens, Gabriel Charles Dante changed his name to the one with which the world soon became familiar.

The budding artist allowed his personal life to influence his interpretation of certain Dantesque episodes, in ways which were at times pleasingly creative, not least because he avoided the manic interpretations of his father. Like his father, the young Dante Gabriel was a rebel of a kind, opposing the artistic establishment represented by Royal Academy conservatives such as Joshua ('Sloshua') Reynolds. He formed a club of fellow-rebels, and in the mysteriously named PRB they were able to make fun of secret associations like those which obsessed Gabriele. Only later did the group reveal that the monogram represented not 'Please Ring Bell' or 'Penis Rather Better', but 'Pre-Raphaelite Brotherhood'.

There was, however, one discovery connected with his father's research which Dante Gabriel exploited well – the discovery by Seymour Kirkup, in the Bargello chapel in 1840, of Giotto's portrait of a youthful Dante. This was transmitted via Rossetti père to Charles Lyell, who publicized it in his 1842 translations of the poems of *Vita nova* and *Convivio* (Fig. 44). This was most important for the young Rossetti. It gave new meaning and

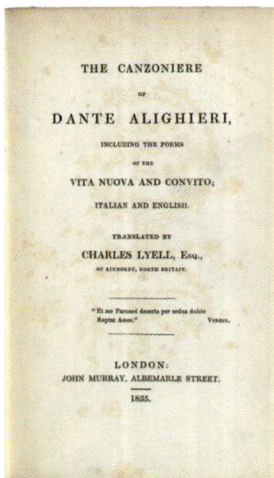

THE CANZONIERE
OF
DANTE ALIGHIERI,
INCLUDING THE POEMS
OF THE
VITA NUOVA AND CONVITO;
ITALIAN AND ENGLISH.

TRANSLATED BY
CHARLES LYELL, Esq.,
OF KINNORDY, NORTH BRITAIN.

"Ei me Parnasi deserta per ardua dulcis
Raptat Amor."   VIRGIL.

LONDON:
JOHN MURRAY, ALBEMARLE STREET,
1835.

45.
Dante Gabriel Rossetti,
*Dante drawing an Angel on
the Anniversary of Beatrice's
Death* (1853), where Dante's
features are modelled
on the Bargello portrait.
Ashmolean Museum,
Oxford.

credibility to the love lyrics of the *Vita nova*, for here was a portrait, not of
an embittered and crusty old man, but of a handsome youth who could
fall in love with the beautiful Beatrice and render the text of *Vita nova* a
believable love story, rather than an allegorical overture to the *Commedia*. It
was to the *Vita nova* that Dante Gabriel dedicated his best efforts in the field
of Dante studies, translating its poems into beautiful English verse (1861),
and deriving from it inspiration and subject-matter for some of his best
paintings. In turn the paintings had an immediate effect upon John Ruskin,
who urged Dante Gabriel to continue with his Dantesque compositions, and
used his own reputation in the London art world to give Rossetti enormous
publicity that enhanced the monetary value of his work.

One of Ruskin's early favourites was a well-known scene from the *Vita nova*
in which the youthful-looking Dante Alighieri, meditating on the anniversary
of Beatrice's death, had drawn a picture of an angel (1853) (Fig. 45). Absorbed
in the written text, and deep in thought for his dead Beatrice, the Poet failed
to observe guests who had entered the room and who had been watching
him at work. He apologizes for being distracted: 'Another was with me.'[113]
Twelve years later it was just such a meditation upon the real death of his wife
Elizabeth Siddal that led Dante Gabriel to create his masterpiece (in its Tate
Gallery version), significantly entitled *Beata Beatrix*. It was in effect a celebration
of his dead wife, modelling the features of 'Beatrice' upon Elizabeth Siddal's
death mask (Fig. 46). If Dante Gabriel could take inspiration for his painting
technique from the painters who preceded Raphael, he could also emulate the
great love story of the earlier Dante Alighieri.

Another significant piece of inspiration (and a further indication of
the way he traced his own emotions to the past), led to Dante Gabriel's 1855

finished version of *Beatrice at a Marriage Feast, denying her Salutation to Dante*, from the *Vita nova* (Fig. 47). Years earlier he had sketched the scene in which Dante Alighieri is described as being ignored or scorned by his beloved Beatrice. The medieval courtly love tradition saw in the withdrawal of the beloved's greeting a sign of disapproval, usually of a moral kind. Dante Gabriel was much more down-to-earth, and a footnote at this point in his translation stresses not some medieval convention, but rather a sensual love such as the young artist would have felt – the sensual love of the young Alighieri for his true beloved, Beatrice, now lost to him forever because of her marriage that day to another. To add a further personal note, the Beatrice figure in the painting was once again modelled on Dante Gabriel's own wife, Elizabeth Siddal. He wrote:

> It is difficult not to connect Dante's agony at this wedding-feast with our knowledge that in her twenty-first year Beatrice was wedded to Simone de' Bardi. That she herself was the bride on this occasion might seem out of the question from the fact of its not being in any way so stated, but, on the other hand, Dante's silence throughout the *Vita nuova* as regards her marriage (which must have brought sorrow even to his ideal love) is so startling that we might almost be led to conceive in this passage the only intimation of it which he thought fit to give.[114]

Dante Gabriel's less ethereal view of marital love and family life is reinforced in his depiction of *La donna della finestra* ('The Lady of the Window'). He translates the relevant lines from *Vita nova*: 'a young and very beautiful lady, who was gazing upon me from a window with a gaze full of pity' (*Vita nova*, 36). The pity stems from the fact that Beatrice had died the year before, and Dante Alighieri derives solace from this compassionate observer. The Lady of the Window had always been a controversial figure for interpreters of this section of the *Vita nova*, most of whom equated her with the consoling power of Philosophy. Once more the down-to-earth Dante Gabriel found no such difficulty in interpretation: the consoling influence of the Lady is for him nothing if not wifely, and in a rare footnote, he adds his own hypothesis:

> Boccaccio tells us that Dante was married to Gemma Donati about a year after the death of Beatrice. Can Gemma then be 'the lady of the window' [...]? Such a passing conjecture would of course imply an admission of what I believe to lie at the heart of all true Dantesque commentary, that is the existence always of the actual events even where the allegorical superstructure has been raised by Dante himself.[115]

47.
Dante Gabriel Rossetti,
*Beatrice at a marriage Feast
denying her Salutation to Dante*
(1855), Ashmolean Museum,
Oxford.

Rossetti's love for his wife Elizabeth Siddal inspired some of his tenderest and most sensuous poetry, in *The House of Life* (part 1870, part 1881). It was the fact that Rossetti thought it healthy to discuss the blessings of conjugal love which, in that hypocritical moral atmosphere of the Victorian era, so aroused the narrow-minded prurience and puritanism of Robert Buchanan (1841–1901). Buchanan's polemic on contemporary poetry laid emphasis on Dante Gabriel's work to the great distress of Rossetti, his friends, and family (and to the detriment of his health and ultimately his life).[116]

Dante Gabriel extended that love for his wife spontaneously and uninhibitedly to his poetry and to his translation, treating Dante Alighieri's Beatrice as a similarly living beloved whom, Dante Gabriel believed, the Poet was not afraid to mention in earthly terms. Rossetti had created a critical view which at once idealized and sensualized conjugal love, interpreting Dante's autobiographical portrait as a reflection of certain aspects of his own life, and impressing on Dante's chaste and literary love some of the more physical and sentimental values of his own marriage to Lizzy Siddal.

Rossetti went on to paint many other episodes and personages from Dante's works, but none reflected the biographical affinity which he felt for the young Alighieri so much as the events narrated in the *Vita nova*. Indeed, Pre-Raphaelite taste was a major factor behind the rise in popularity of

Dante's minor work, which counted four complete translations into English
by 1862. Had his father been alive to see the results of his son's efforts he
would no doubt have been alarmed, not only at the absence of any sectarian
interpretations of the text, but even more at the Victorian domesticity
of certain reaches of Dante Gabriele's beautiful translation. While the
elder Rossetti's far-fetched theories never gained currency in British Dante
scholarship, Dante Gabriel's translations, poetry, paintings and drawings
ensured that the Pre-Raphaelite version of Dante, particularly of certain
episodes from the *Vita nova*, holds even today a powerful position in the
realm of Dante iconography.

CHAPTER 7

Paget Toynbee's Dante collection

Diego Zancani

Paget Jackson Toynbee, a well-known name in Dante scholarship, was born in Wimbledon on 20 January 1855. After attending Haileybury School he read Classics at Oxford, as a member of Balliol College (1874–78), and then travelled to India, Japan and Australia, working mainly as a private tutor. He had visited Italy earlier, and Italian landscapes were on his mind even in Japan, where on 13 April 1887 he sent a postcard to his friend W. P. Ker:

> I am writing this in a Buddhist priest's house at the top of a mountain covered with huge pines & cryptomerias – a sort of Japanese Vallombrosa – in the midst of the most sacred temples in Japan. Very few Europeans have as yet penetrated here and are objects of great curiosity to the natives.[117]

After he returned to Britain he became interested in Romance philology and edited an anthology of early French texts,[118] followed by an English adaptation of a French historical grammar[119]. But his real interest lay in the works of Dante Alighieri, and in 1898 he published his most famous work, *A Dictionary of Proper Names and Notable Matters in the Works of Dante*. This was very successful and went through numerous editions, the last one appearing as recently as 1968 (Fig. 48).[120] In 1876 Edward Moore, one of the leading Dante scholars in Oxford, founded the Oxford Dante Society, which undoubtedly gave academic sanction to the 'cult' of Dante in Britain. Toynbee became a member of the Society in 1895 and later its secretary, from 1916 until 1928. He continued to write on Dante, apart from a period after his wife's death in 1910, when he completed the edition of Walpole's letters initiated by Mrs Toynbee.[121] He received numerous accolades and was made a Fellow of the British Academy and a corresponding member of the Cambridge (USA) Dante Society, founded in 1881; of the Istituto Lombardo di Scienze e Lettere; of the Accademia Lucchese; and in 1917 he was made

48.
Photo of title page from *A Dictionary of Proper Names and Notable Matters in the Works of Dante* (new edition), by Paget Jackson Toynbee, edited and revised by Charles Singleton, the great American Dantist (Oxford, 1968). Oxford, Bodleian Library, 28521 d.170.

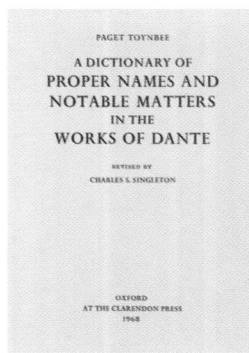

PAGET TOYNBEE

A DICTIONARY OF
PROPER NAMES AND
NOTABLE MATTERS
IN THE
WORKS OF DANTE

REVISED BY
CHARLES S. SINGLETON

OXFORD
AT THE CLARENDON PRESS
1968

a member of the Accademia della Crusca. Partly because of ill health (he suffered from the consequences of typhoid fever) he became a recluse in the house he had built, Fiveways, in the village of Burnham in Buckinghamshire, where he died in 1932.

In order to understand the reasons for Toynbee's fascination with Dante, it will be necessary to reconstruct the intellectual milieu in Oxford between approximately 1865, the sixth centenary of Dante's birth, and the early part of the twentieth century. when a large number of scholars became professionally interested in the works of the Florentine poet and especially in the text and criticism of the *Commedia*. The contribution to the establishment of an essentially critical text of Dante's works reached its peak with the publication of the so-called 'Oxford Dante' by Edward Moore in 1894. This had an index of names prepared by Paget Toynbee, later expanded into his 1898 *Dictionary of Proper Names and Notable Matters in the Works of Dante*.[122] This 1894 Oxford edition was the first time all of Dante's works had been published in a single volume, and one of the first occasions when Oxford University Press had produced a foreign-language volume not in one of the classical languages (Fig. 49).

A serious interest in Dante's works had already been shown by prominent figures in Oxford: in 1835 by William Ewart Gladstone, who made some partial translations from the *Commedia* in *terza rima*, and in 1840 by the Rev. John Keble, the Professor of Poetry, who devoted some of his Latin lectures to an appreciation of Dante, comparing him to Lucretius. Even more important for Dante's Oxford fortunes was the interest shown by John Ruskin, especially in the second and third volumes of his *Modern Painters*.[123] Ruskin had become acquainted with the *Commedia* during a visit to Italy in 1845, and he never failed to show his appreciation of it thereafter. In the third volume of his *Stones of Venice* (1853) he wrote: 'I think that the central man of all the world, as representing in perfect balance the imaginative, moral, and intellectual faculties, all at their highest, is Dante.'[124] Toynbee remarked that 'There can be no doubt that Ruskin's whole-hearted appreciation of the *Commedia*, so insistently and so eloquently expressed in his numerous works, has played no small part in awakening and stimulating the widespread interest in this country in the study of Dante.'[125]

Although a keen interest in Dante in Oxford circles can be traced back to the early years of the nineteenth century, the chronological limits of this partial study will be the two anniversary years 1865 and 1921. It would be impossible to delve here into the intellectual, religious and political reasons why Dante became the centre of attention especially (but certainly not exclusively) in Oxford in this period. However, we can find ample testimony to Toynbee's passion for Dante not only in his numerous articles, editions and books, but also among his correspondence, some of which has survived in the Bodleian Library, with some scattered letters and postcards preserved

49.
Tutte le opere di Dante Alighieri, nuovamente rivedute nel testo da Edward Moore (Oxford, 1894), inside back cover. The 'Oxford Dante', with autograph notes by Toynbee, mostly on typographical errors. Oxford, Bodleian Library, Toynbee 2805.

in books bequeathed by him to his college. These documents reveal the vast network of correspondents with whom he exchanged detailed information concerning problems of interpretation, philological minutiae, textual *cruces*, and a general enthusiasm for the author of the *Commedia*. Soon after graduation, in the 1880s, he had started collecting early editions of Dante, Petrarch, and Boccaccio, and among his earliest acquisitions we find the following: a *Commedia* with the commentary of Landino and Vellutello (Venice: Giovambattista Marchio Sessa et fratelli, 1564) and *La Visione: poema di Dante Alighieri* (Padova: Donato Pasquardi et compagno, 1629), both bought in Florence in 1883 from the Franchi bookshop; a *Vita Nuova con XV canzoni del medesimo* (Firenze: Sermartelli, 1576), bought in Paris in 1891, together with *Il Petrarcha* (Vinegia: Aldo Romano, 1514); and a copy of Boccaccio's *Laberinto d'amore* (Venezia: Nicolino da Sabio, 1536), bought in Paris in 1894 along with a copy of *Ameto* (Venetia: Giovan Battista Bonfadio, 1586).

However, the bulk of his acquisitions took place after 1898, presumably thanks to the extra income generated by the *Dictionary of Proper Names*. About 272 books, including a few duplicates, of works by Boccaccio, Petrarch, and Dante were listed in Toynbee's own hand in a register entitled *Catalogue of the Library of Paget Toynbee, M.A., D. Litt., Coll Ball. Oxon. 'Dante, Petrarca, Boccaccio'*,[126] with the date and place of acquisition and an indication of the price paid for each book. He frequently referred to this as his 'Dante Collection'. In some of his correspondence we also find specific reference to the ways Toynbee acquired his books: he used to contact well-known antiquarian booksellers in various countries, such as Romagnoli and Zanichelli in Bologna; Benedetti in Rome; Hoepli in Milan; Olschki, Davis & Orioli, Franchi and Seeber in Florence; Silvio Moro in Udine; Di Giuseppe in Naples; and Sangiorgi in Venice; and after they sent him a catalogue he would order the book in which he was interested. Soon, however, the booksellers themselves would offer him works by Dante, Petrarch, and Boccaccio, by sending him a postcard. In France he bought his books mainly in Paris from Emile Paul, Welter and Gamber, and at specific sales. In Germany he bought from Rosenthal in Munich and from List & Francke in Leipzig. In Britain he bought one book from Young in Liverpool; one in Birmingham, Bristol, Reading, Leeds, and Oxford; and approximately 59 in London.[127]

From the beginning it was Toynbee's intention to donate most of his books to the Bodleian Library. He gave approximately 360 works in 1912, 375 in 1913, about 350 in 1916 and about 700 in 1917, with a further 600 volumes in 1923. Approximately 1,400 books were donated after his death in 1932,[128] making a total of nearly 4,000 books overall.[129] The University was very grateful for Toynbee's gift, and in 1913 a formal decree of thanks was issued by the Vice-Chancellor, Charles Buller Heberden, Principal of Brasenose and himself a Dante scholar. Falconer Madan, Bodley's Librarian, was enthusiastic about the donation, which enriched considerably the holdings of Oxford University's library. In a letter to Toynbee he wrote:

> All the chief Dante Scholars alive are connected with Oxford.
> You, the Vice-Chancellor, Shadwell, Moore, W. W. Jackson,
> Tozer. What does it matter if we have duplicates. We should
> if necessary get rid of *them*, and retain the Toynbee copies.
> What with the Canonici MSS., the Mortara printed books
> and your donations we shall have one of the finest collections
> of the *best* Italian literature in Christendom.[130]

Although numerous books in the collection are by Petrarch and Boccaccio,[131] I shall concentrate mainly on the editions of Dante's works. Toynbee collected various editions of the *Convivio*; one was a precious copy from the collection of the Duke of Sussex,[132] published in Florence by Bonaccorsi in 1490,[133] and two copies of the same work, printed in Venice by Zuane Antonio e Fratelli da Sabio in 1521 (Fig 40), plus four copies of the Venetian edition by Nicolo di Aristotile Zoppino (1529), and one by Marchio Sessa (1531), plus the *Convito* and a *Vita Nuova* (Venice: Pietro Gatti, 1793). The *Vita nova* is also represented by the first printed edition (Florence: B. Sermartelli, 1576) and a few nineteenth-century editions, among which the rare first English translation of this work, which appeared in *The Early Life of Dante Alighieri together with the Original in Parallel Pages* by Joseph Garrow Esq. (Florence: Felix Le Monnier, 1846). Dante's *Rime* are represented by four copies of the Florentine Giunta edition (1527), and two of the Venetian one (Io. Antonio e Fratelli da Sabio, 1532).

The *Commedia* is, of course, present in numerous editions:

Venice, Octaviano Scoto da Monza, 1484 (imperfect)

Venice, Pietro Cremonese ditto Veronese, 1491 (imperfect)

Venice, Bernardino Benali, 1491

Venice, Mattheo di Chodeca da Parma, 1493

Venice, Aldus Manutius, 1502

Florence, Philippo di Giunta, 1506

Toscolano, Alex. Pag. Benacenses, 1506 [?] (two copies)

Venice, Bartholomeo da Zanni da Portese, 1507

Venice, Bernardino Stagnino da Trino de Monferra, 1512

Venice, Aldus Manutius, 1515

Venice, Bernardino Stagnino da Trino de Monfera, 1520

Venice, Jacob del Burgofranco, 1529

Venice, Bernardino Stagnino ad instantia di Giovanni Giolito da Trino, 1536

Venice, Francesco Marcolini, 1544 (Fig. 39)

Lyon, Giovan di Tormes, 1547

Lyon, Guglielmo Rovillio, 1551 (two copies)

Lyon, Guglielmo Rovillio, 1552

Venice, Gabriel Giolito de' Ferrari e fratelli, 1555 (Fig. 9)

Venice, Giovambattista Marchio Sessa et fratelli, 1564

Venice, Pietro da Fino, 1568

Lyon, Guglielmo Rovillio, 1571

Venice, Giovambattista Marchio Sessa et fratelli, 1578

Florence, Domenico Manzani, 1595

Venice, Gio. Battista e Gio. Bernardo Sessa Fratelli, 1596

Padova, Donato Pasquardi et compagno, 1629

Toynbee owned two copies of the earliest printed edition of the *Monarchia* (Basel: Joannes Oporinus [Johann Herbst], 1559), and in December 1907 he presented one of them to the British Museum Library. A copy of

De la volgare eloquenzia (Vicenza: Janicu_o, 1529) was given to W. W. Vernon
on 5 September 1900, but Toynbee ke⊃t a second copy, indicating that this
edition also contained Trissino's *Poetica* and *Castellano*. The edition with the
Latin text was printed in Paris, 'Apud Io. Corbin, 1577',[134] and three copies of
the Ferrara edition (D. Mamarelli, 158_) are also recorded.[135]

Among Petrarch's works, apart from those already mentioned, we find *Le
opere volgari* (Venice: Lazaro Soardo, 15__); the *Canzoniere* with the commentary
by Francesco Filelfo and Antonio da Tempo (Venice: Bernardino Stagnino
alias de Ferrariis de Tridino Montifferati, 1522); *Le volgari opere del Petrarca con
la esposizione di Alessandro Vellutello* (Venice: Giovannantonio e fratelli da Sabbio,
1525); *Il Petrarca col commento di M. Sebastiano Fausto da Longiano* (Venice: Francesco
di Alessandro Bindoni e Mapheo Pasini, 1532); *Il Petrarca col commento di Sylvano
da Venaphro* (Naples: Antonio Jovino et Matthio Canzer, 1533). Toynbee was
clearly interested in the early Petrarch commentaries, even the ones which
were not very reliable and were criticized by contemporary readers, like the
one by Francesco Filelfo (Fig. 21). Over twenty-five later editions are also
listed in Toynbee's collection.

Approximately 132 copies of works by Boccaccio are listed, the largest
number being editions of *Fiammetta* (27), *De casibus*, and *De claris mulieribus*,
frequently in Italian translations (36 copies in total), *Corbaccio* — also known
as *Laberinto d'Amore* — (20), *Filocolo* and *Ameto* (14 and 12, respectively), *De
montibus* (6, including a few incunables), *Urbano* (4), as well as 9 copies of
the *Decameron*. Most of the books are in octavo, but a copy of the *Decameron*
published in Venice by Gabriel Giolito de Ferrari (1546) is in quarto, and
came from the Sunderland Library at Blenheim.

In addition to his substantial donation made to Bodley, Toynbee gave a
small number of books to Balliol College library — about 40 early editions
of Italian texts, plus all his own printed works, and the letters of Horace
Walpole edited by Mrs Toynbee.[136] Among these is a copy of the *Decameron*
(Florence: heredi di Philippo Giunta, 1527) bought in London at Thorp's in
March 1925 for £12. 10s, which contains numerous manuscript annotations,
some in French and in English, and an attempt to change the text according
to the expurgated version, in which the 'angel Gabriel' becomes 'the king of
the fairies', the word for 'bishop' is substituted by 'knight' and the name of
God is substituted by 'Nature'.

The material contained in the Toynbee manuscripts in the Bodleian
Library and in most of the offprints bound in two volumes,[137] as well as
in the newspaper cuttings collected by Paget Toynbee,[138] demonstrates
the contacts between Toynbee and some of the best-known Dantists in
the world. In 1890 he received the rare Aldine Bembo edition of Dante's
Commedia (Venice: Aldus Manutius, 1502) as a wedding gift from Arthur
John Butler,[139] professor of Italian at University College London (see Fig.
38).[140] In fact Toynbee kept a meticulous record of everything, including

receipts for his purchases. The names that appear most frequently among his correspondents include: W. W. Vernon, Edward Moore, H. F. Tozer, W. W. Jackson, C. L. Shadwell,[141] C. B. Heberden, and many scholars from Italy (Francesco Torraca, Pio Rajna, Flaminio Pellegrini), Germany, and America, especially Charles Norton.

An examination of the selections made by Toynbee in his 1907 anthology *In the Footprints of Dante*,[142] will help to establish the criteria, largely shared by scholars and readers, for creating a Dante 'canon' in Britain. The passages from the *Commedia* are numerous, but preference is given to famous similes, to essentially lyrical passages, to 'atmospheric' moments. Basically these are the same passages that the majority of Italian students read in their secondary schools. The choice of translation is also indicative: although there are many passages translated by Cary, and some by Rossetti, there are none by Longfellow. The anthology, like most of Toynbee's work, represents a no-nonsense, concrete approach to Dante with a discussion of detailed issues which help to clarify an essential understanding of the poetry. He frequently discusses why a rare textual variant (frequently a *lectio difficilior*) is to be preferred: for example, *sollenare* meaning 'alleviate' is preferable to the variant *sollevare*, although in 1829 it was completely misunderstood as *solennare* ('to make solemn') in two passages of the *Vita nova* (chapters 20 and 40).[143] There is no trace of ideological prejudice, virtually no polemicizing, in Toynbee's work, just verifiable facts as found in existing texts, and in reputable scholarship.

Another important essay by Toynbee, on 'Oxford and Dante', was contributed to the miscellaneous volume *Dante. Essays in Commemoration 1321–1921*. Starting from the earliest mention of Oxford in connection with Dante, namely by Giovanni da Serravalle, bishop of Fermo, in his Latin commentary on the *Commedia* (1416–17), who believed Dante had visited the English city, Toynbee diligently follows the translations, the commentaries and the discussions of Dante connected with Oxford. They reach a peak in 1876 with the creation of the Dante Society by Rev. Edward Moore, Principal of St Edmund Hall, with Signor de Tivoli, Taylorian teacher in Italian, Rev. H. F. Tozer of Exeter College, Rev. G. W. Kitchin of Christ Church, and Rev. R. G. Livingstone of Pembroke, 'an event' – as Toynbee remarked – 'which gave an impulse to the study of Dante in Oxford, and consequentially far beyond the limits of Oxford, that has lasted unimpaired to the present day'.[144] Toynbee mentions Duke Humphrey's donation to the University library in 1444, which included Serravalle's commentary and a copy of the Italian text of the *Commedia*, the earliest recorded in England (unfortunately now lost). The editions of Dante's *Commedia* owned by the Bodleian Library slowly increased, and in the 1620 catalogue five were listed. In 1746 'the first Oxford specimen of translation from the *Commedia*' (*Inf. XXIV.* 1–18) appeared anonymously, but made by Joseph Spence,

Fellow of New College. In 1792 Henry Francis Cary, a student at Christ Church, showed an interest in translating into prose a few passages from the *Commedia*. In January 1797 Cary wrote in his journal that he had begun work on his blank verse translation, which was to be finished in May 1812, and published in 1814.[145]

In the Bodleian printed catalogue of 1843 there are thirteen editions of the *Commedia* recorded – seven incunables, including the *editio princeps* of Foligno (1472), and the first Florentine edition (1481), plus six sixteenth-century ones. Editions of the *Monarchia* (1559) and *Vita nova* (1576) are also mentioned for the first time. Toynbee quotes an anonymous article (written by Rev. Samuel Henry Reynolds, Fellow and tutor of Brasenose) in the *Westminster Review* of 1861 on 'Dante and his English Translators', in which it is stated that 'Dante is certainly more studied now than he has been for very long'. Translations are increasing and critical works, 'some of them of a very high order', are being published, but, Reynolds remarks, 'the change, whatever its cause may be, has been quite recent: it would hardly be untrue to say that there is more of Dante's influence traceable in Chaucer's poems – more genuine evidence that Dante had been read and loved – than in the whole body of English literature (Milton's writings alone excepted) from Chaucer's time to our own'.[146] It is well known that the renewed interest in Dante's works in Britain is bound up with the political enthusiasm in England for Italian unification, which came about in 1861; one might add that politics and religion, two themes very close to Dante's heart, clearly played a part in Dante's revival. It is not by chance that some of the prominent figures in the cultural life of the English capital in the second half of the nineteenth century, such as Antonio Panizzi and Gabriele Rossetti, contributed to the cause of the Risorgimento. Panizzi apparently worked very closely – basically as a secret agent – for the Piedmontese prime minister, Camillo Benso di Cavour, after they met in 1852. Panizzi's friendship with Gladstone and his influence as Keeper of Printed Books and Principal Librarian at the British Museum was a crucial link between literature and politics.[147]

William Gladstone, a former student of Christ Church, had some of his translations from *Purgatorio* and *Paradiso*, made in 1835, and a short translation from *Inferno*, made in 1837, published in 1861, when he was Chancellor of the Exchequer. Matthew Arnold, an old member of Balliol College and a Fellow of Oriel, published an essay on 'Dante and Beatrice', in *Fraser's Magazine*, in 1863.[148] This last topic would be one of the themes dear to a quintessentially Oxonian brotherhood, the Pre-Raphaelites.[149]

While in Italy there were numerous events to celebrate the six-hundredth anniversary of Dante's birth, in Oxford, John Dayman published a *terza rima* translation of the whole *Commedia* (1865), and a translation of the *Inferno* was published by the Rev. James Ford, who completed the whole poem in 1870.[150]

Toynbee also mentions that in 1865 a subject relating to Dante was selected for the Latin verse prize at Oxford, namely 'Dantis Exsilium', and that the prize was won by a Balliol student, R. B. Michell. He does not make any remarks about the merit of the winner, but in 1913 he received a letter from Lord Kilbracken which threw serious doubts on the award:

> The subject of the Latin Verse Prize Poem at Oxford, 1865 was 'Dante's Exilium'. But if you should by chance hear of it, I strongly advise you not to spend sixpence on it. It is a very poor performance. It is by R. Michell of Balliol, son of the late Principal of Magdalen Hall, afterwards Hertford College; this dignitary held the Office of Public Orator and, as such, was one of the examiners for the Latin Verse Prize, to which fact I cannot but attribute his son's success – viewing the quality of the poem. You shall see it, if you like, when you come here. Old Michell, like Habakkuk, was 'capable de tout', as I daresay you know.[151]

In 1872 a substantial essay by a well-known scholar, John Addington Symonds, formerly a Fellow of Magdalen College, was published with the title *Introduction to the Study of Dante*; it had a second edition in 1890. In 1874 the Clarendon Press published for the first time a volume on Dante, namely the *Selections from the 'Inferno'*, edited by H. B. Cotterill. In 1876, as we have seen, the Oxford Dante Society was founded and is still in existence. In the 1870s and 1880s the major libraries in Oxford and Dr Edward Moore bought important Dante manuscripts, and in 1886 Moore was appointed to the Barlow Lectureship on Dante at University College London: his massive *Contributions to the Textual Criticism of the 'Divina Commedia'* was published by Cambridge University Press in 1889. From then on, the works of Moore, Toynbee, and Vernon in particular continued to keep Dante at the forefront of literary studies. In 1917 the last series of Edward Moore's *Studies in Dante* was published. Further activity was promoted in this field for the centenary year 1921, and in Italy there were various events to celebrate the sixth centenary of Dante's death, including a pageant in Florence and the re-discovery and re-burial of his bones in Ravenna, as Toynbee, himself relates.[152]

The Italian edition of Dante's works that Toynbee was reading in 1921 contained a first draft of the 'critical text' established by the Società Dantesca Italiana and the texts were edited by all the major Italian scholars of the time: M. Barbi, E. G. Parodi, F. Pellegrini, E. Pistelli, P. Rajna, E. Rostagno, G. Vandelli, with an analytical index compiled by Mario Casella.[153] The fact that Toynbee was asked to write a review of it for the *Times Literary Supplement* proves the standing in which he was held. Although the 'Oxford

Dante' is not mentioned in the preface to the Società Dantesca volume, its achievements must have been well known to the Italian scholarly community. The seriousness of Toynbee's work on Dante, his 'long study and great love' (*Inf.* I. 83) was widely recognized, not only in Britain where he was called 'a giant of scholarship',[154] but also by numerous eminent Dantists in Italy.[155] Most of them had, after all, corresponded with him, and especially in their letters written in Italian, there is frequently a tone of great deference and admiration for Dr Toynbee.

Toynbee's intellect was particularly directed towards factual questions, rather than being interested in aesthetic or stylistic questions. But this practical approach produced the first useful Dante research tool (the list of proper names in the 'Oxford Dante', and the later dictionary), as well as other surveys: *Dante in English Literature from Chaucer to Cary (c. 1380-1844)* (London, 1909); the *Chronological List of English Translations from Dante, from Chaucer to the Present Day* (1906, in his *Dante Studies*, Oxford, 1921); and, for the Dante Centenary, *Britain's Tribute to Dante in Literature and Art. A Chronological Record of 540 Years (c. 1380–1920)* (London, 1921). However, Paget Toynbee also made a vital philological contribution to Dante studies, particularly in the important 1920 edition of the Latin letters, on which the 1921 Italian centenary edition was based;[156] and by leaving for posterity his huge legacy of manuscripts and printed editions of works by the *Tre Corone*, especially Dante.

CHAPTER 8

Hershey Heaven and Dante's Hell

Tom Phillips

When I started work on the *Inferno* I was, in my mid-thirties, just the right age, i.e. *nel mezzo del cammin di nostra vita*. Now, invited to participate both visually and verbally in a Dante exhibition and symposium, I am jolted awake to find myself (numerically at least) twice half-way through this journey of our life. I only hope there is some road left.

It seems an appropriate moment to take a backward glance.[157] Sorting out one's archive licenses solipsism. It is not an accident that I snatched as my motto Beckett's wonderful prescription (from *Worstword Ho*), 'No matter. Try again. Fail again. Fail better'. I permit myself to feel that in making my version of the *Inferno* I could not have pondered or invented more, or worked harder, or more diligently explored a graphic repertoire or exploited the technical means available at the time. In short I could not, within my given means, have failed better.

All our performances, of course, are creatures of their epoch; but it is possible that the 1970s and 80s were ideal times of stylistic freedom. In what genre was I working? I begin to suspect, and am told, that in the allusive conflation of word and image my work exemplifies that chimera called post-modernism. To have been one of the defining visionaries of a mirage, *il miglior fabbro* of a fault line in cultural discourse and the exemplar of a hiccup in art history, is a strange ambition and a stranger fate: yet it has been, and I confess, still is, 'all my calling / until that certain curtain's final falling'.[158]

If, however, mirages can be brought into focus Dante did just that for me. The resultant book is freighted with my world of armchair reference plus every device and strategy of art I had up to then explored. One piece of baggage had to be left behind since music, except for the bugled fart that ends *Inferno* XXI, is (by God's implied decree) absent from Hell (Fig. 50).

It is only now that I realize, as I look through the archive of proofs and tests and transparencies, that this lack of music and its means matched exactly what I was attempting visually to supply. Having worked on opera libretti, I see an analogy between setting a text for the opera stage and illuminating it for the pages of a book via harmony and discord, finding the appropriate *tessitura* for an image, searching out the thematic and motivic links in Dante's text, using the spectrum from soloistic black and white to full polychromatic orchestration (as in the frontispiece of 'Dante in his Study', which uses 26 colour printings) (Fig. 51). From that perspective my fragments of treated text can be seen as a counterpoint to the facing pages of translation, or an *obbligato* commentary.

Delayed realization of such a process demonstrates how little was consciously willed. I stood on mighty shoulders. All was brought about by Dante's own marked map of human life, ever pointing to something in my experience or summoning up some piece of forgotten knowledge or signposting some graphic experiment.

50.
Tom Phillips, *Inferno* XXI:
Bugled Fart

Beginning with the translation, this was taxing work; but in all its stages there was 'Hershey Heaven', and more of it than I have experienced since. This mysterious phrase was unknown to me when I was struggling with Dante but, once encountered, cast its light back on that strange rapture in toil that is the artist's privilege.

The term cropped up when I was painting the portrait of Nobel laureate Sir John Sulston for Pembroke College, Cambridge (Fig. 52). As we talked during the sittings, he would try to explain to me the concept of the genome. I was concentrating on making a picture at the same time and never quite grasped the details. What I did learn, however, is how a scientist's activity parallels that of an artist. One such similarity is Hershey

Heaven. To paraphrase Alfred Hershey (via Alan Garen via John Sulston), this occurs when a task is exacting and laborious and driven by time and consists of repeated laboratory/studio processes which are yielding results. In Hershey Heaven the work is always there to greet you, ready each day for you to resume. You don't have to think up what to do or justify your efforts, just get on with the perseverant job; another few lines of the translation or corrections of its umpteenth draft, another thousand dots on a lithograph or some cross-hatching on an etching plate. Nonetheless it is an essential part of the creative act, since the dogged rigour it demands is a test of an idea's strength. Somehow it's like transcendental knitting. One day, alas, the end of the intricate scarf is reached and the job is done. Hershey Heaven is once more postponed. You are back to a dark and puzzling wood, imagining, planning and improvising, seeking a new road which, if it is right, will lead again (*a riveder le stelle*) to that same bliss.

John Sulston showed me the drawings, each numbered and dated (à la Picasso), that he made when working on the genome of the nematode worm. Identical in format and calligraphy, they were coloured clusters of roundish shapes. Part of me wondered why scientists, who think nothing of commandeering millions for the latest sophistication of their equipment, can't scrape together a pound or two for a pen that does not leak or stutter or make blobby marks. In all other respects I was fascinated by the sequence

52.
Tom Phillips, Study for portrait of John Sulston after his ms notes

of hundreds upon hundreds of these observational transcriptions of what goes on inside the tiny and transparent worm, as seen through the microscope with the aid of a cunningly prepared slide (on which the worm lives a life of customized luxury that would gain the admiration of animal rightists, if they cared about worms).

One of these sheets of life drawings included a sequence partly crossed out with the words 'try again' written by the side. It was this echo of Beckett that made me use the drawings for the whole background of the portrait, thereby haloing John Sulston with his own Hershey Heaven.

———————

I once tried to remember where and when I first collided with Dante's *Inferno* and assumed it must have been at school in the middle of a standard binge on Penguin Classics. It was only when I was talking with my mother a few years before her death that I was reminded of a much earlier and more artistically formative encounter. When I was five or six my brother and I, both keen Cubs, wheeled a home-made cart around the streets of Clapham collecting books to be pulped for the war effort. Most were ordinary enough. In one house, however, the proffered volumes were noticeably bigger and better and the grandest of them all was a huge, sumptuous object bound in red and gold and containing scary black-and-white pictures. This was Doré's version of the *Inferno.* We kept it guiltily around the house for a while before eventually consigning it to what then seemed its better future, as ration books. Once my memory was jogged I recalled the sneaked glimpses at the hair-raising plates of the semi-forbidden book, placed by my mother on a high shelf because of its too frequent portrayals of naked flesh. It was strange to think that (to paraphrase my favourite Glen Baxter cartoon) my first brush with art, in a pictureless home, should occur at the same time as my first meeting with a work that would later dominate fifteen years of my life. The Norns are up early weaving one's rope of destiny.

When I read the *Inferno* at school, as a more than usually pretentious fifth-former, I seem to remember finding it (in Dorothy L. Sayers's translation) disappointingly parochial. Thus I had missed the point entirely, as I discovered later when studying the original with the aid of Singleton's copiously annotated crib. My later self saw, of course, that these once celebrated nonentities were, like Chaucer's pilgrims and the denizens of Proust's lost time, the eternal and universal figures now immortalized in the phrase 'the usual suspects' (thanks to *Casablanca*), the all too recognizable and emblematic *dramatis personae* of life (oneself included) who cyclically replace themselves. I once asked Samuel Beckett — to talk with whom felt like addressing Virgil — what batsman he had most enjoyed watching. 'Woolley' he said, 'certainly Woolley', mentioning a cricketer who to me was a grainy black-and-white figure, a scarcely remembered run-stealer who flickered to

and fro on the Pathé newsreels. This met in me that almost blank response I see in the eyes of those to whom I now instance the names of Compton and Edrich. They will themselves in their turn one day provoke the same reaction with mention of Flintoff and Pietersen. For encounters with all these, especially Beckett, one must search the *Paradiso* of Wisden.

————————

The initial suggestion that I might illustrate the *Inferno* came in 1975, from an unlikely source. The Folio Society asked Joe Studholme, the director of Editions Alecto, if he knew of a suitable artist to provide drawings to accompany a new translation. My name was put forward, and after agreeing to have a shot at the task I submitted some preliminary ideas which, seemingly, bared the unacceptable face of Modernism. 'These aren't illustrations at all', said the then Mr Folio, and perhaps he was right. He eventually decided unexcitingly to partner Carey's classical blank verse with the lacklustre Flaxman designs printed, unaccountably, in blue.

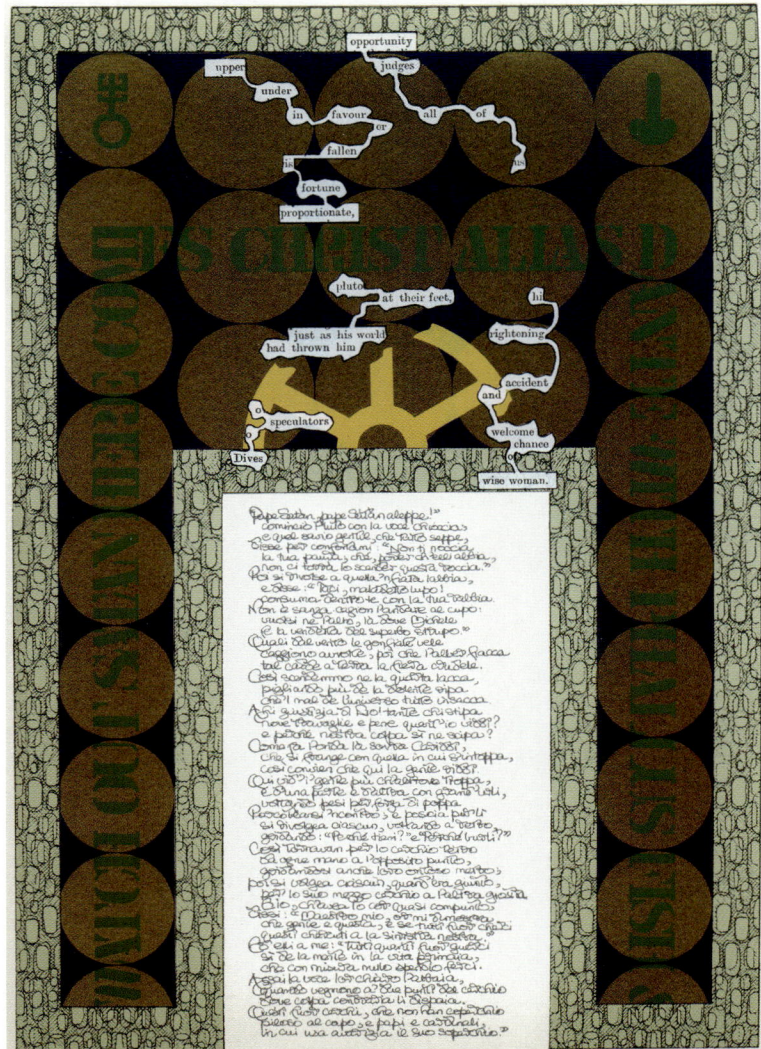

When I mentioned this response to Editions Alecto they proposed
almost at once to undertake the project themselves, in more grandiose
fashion as a full-scale *livre d'artiste* (Fig. 53). I started thinking about what
such a book could be like and cast around for an up-to-date translation.
I failed to find a modern version that echoed what I identified as Dante's
colloquial gravity, and came in any case more and more to feel I had little
right to illustrate a work that I had borrowed rather than, in some sense,
truly possessed. Herr Doktor Gesamtkunstwerk had sprung his trap again
and I was gladly self-condemned to a few hundred evenings struggling
with my own pentameters in draft after draft, the very essence in fact of
Hershey Heaven. Meanwhile, in the lavishly equipped studios of Alecto, I
started experimenting with imagery, with the idea of incorporating into each
plate not only a commentary deriving from Mallock's *A Human Document*

(the source of my own *A Humument*) but also a handwritten version of the original Italian (Fig. 54).

I was naturally aware of the long history of Dante illustration and the many artists who have revelled in the rich pictorial opportunities provided by the poet, especially within the *Inferno*. In the twentieth century both Salvador Dali and Georg Grosz tackled the work, though unfortunately not in their artistic prime. Only Robert Rauschenberg added fresh energies to the tradition (not, however, in book form). In his large silkscreened graphics he invented a visual language full of personal reference worthy of the poem – and, curiously enough, featuring a similarly obsolescent cast of contemporary characters.

Athletes have it easy, for in their events they merely compete with a narrow age-band of the living. In the art Olympics we have to run against the dead, as well – some of whom, though over five hundred years old, are still in great form. In a field which includes all the fine illuminators of early manuscripts, two outstanding contestants are still a lap or so ahead, because each artistically and intellectually matched Dante's own imaginative muscle.

Botticelli, with his supreme draughtsmanship and pictorial organization, has the added grace of seeming to know Dante and Beatrice personally. He draws them as if they were people he saw daily going about the place. When preparing the exhibition of Botticelli's illustrations at the Royal Academy, I had the privilege of handling (albeit with the obligatory white gloves) the originals and was able to scrutinize them closely, only to marvel the more at the purity and confidence of his supple lines.

Even closer in spirit to Dante's harsh eschatology is the compacted vitality of Blake's obsessive visions. These were for me a touchstone, because they provided a robust dialogue with the *Commedia* which makes the work of most predecessors (and successors) look ploddingly literal. In quirky homage I transposed one of Blake's images into the style and high key of an American comic to accompany the *buffo* carnival of devilish combat in canto XXII (Fig. 55). It was interesting to find how little change was necessary, but then the worlds of Superman and the Hulk are not far away from Blake's strange universe of mythic cookery.

I had never, of course, quite forgotten that first encounter with Dante in the form of Doré's monster volume. Now that I more legitimately owned the splendid red heavyweight, its pictures excited me less because Doré has nothing to say beyond the faithful picturing of each episode. What did impress me, however, was the cinematic quality of his cycle of images, as if they were a prototypical storyboard for an epic film. In another age Doré would have made a fine film director along the lines of Cecil B. de Mille or, more exactly, William Dieterle. This was proved in Harry Lachman's 1935 movie *Dante's Inferno* (starring Spencer Tracy and featuring Rita Hayworth's dancing debut). Although the film's title refers in this case to a fairground

55.
Tom Phillips, *Inferno* XXII:
Devils Fighting

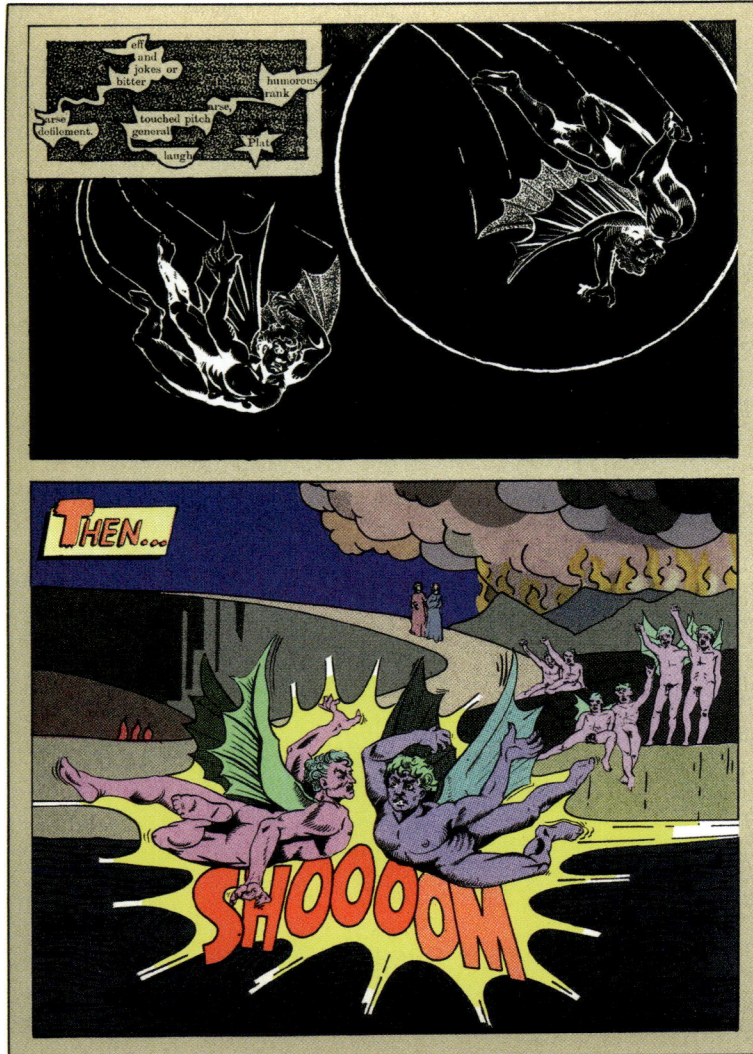

attraction in the genre of Haunted Houses, it includes a ten-minute nightmare sequence in which Lachman, with the help of Willy Pogany, brings Doré's images persuasively to life to frighten the hero into mending his ways (which, being Spencer Tracy, he does).

I also bought a cheap repro edition of Doré's pictures which I thought to cut up as collage material. For this purpose old bound copies of the *Boy's Own Paper* (of roughly the same vintage but on more viable paper) proved more suitable. Here and there, however, small fragments of Doré made their now unidentifiable appearance, as in the background to the figure in canto XXI (see Fig. 50).

But my own Spencer Tracy nightmare was to come. Towards the end of 1978, I received a phone call early one morning to say that a small accidental fire had reached the all-too-combustible chemicals at the print studios of Editions Alecto, resulting in an explosion that had lifted the roof off the workshop and destroyed all but a small batch of proofs of the first year's work on the images. Once over the initial shock, I determined to view this as criticism from above. I decided to start again, this time under my own steam as the book's publisher. The Talfourd Press (named somewhat later after the road in Peckham where I live and work) began rather shakily early in 1979, when I lured Nick Tite from Editions Alecto to be the co-ordinator as well as master-etcher for the venture. This enabled me also to revise my strategies for the pictorial matter, notably to abandon the idea of including Dante's own Italian text in what had become a verbal clutter.

Since I had decided to spare no cost or effort in making the book I now dreamed of, it seemed best to start with the paper. This was made and tinted to my own specification at Inveresk Mills, near Wells in Somerset. I incorporated my signature into the watermark. By what Dame Edna would call a spooky coincidence I later found that the paper mill stood next to land whose rents were once collected by the father of Dante's Beatrice. Moreover, a later Bishop of Wells had written a book suggesting (a likely story) that Dante himself had visited the town since a clock described by him resembled that of the Cathedral.

Whereas countless sheets of paper and whole notebooks were eventually filled with the preparatory textual and visual studies for the work, the back of an envelope seemed to suffice for my optimistically blithe financial calculations. This involved a second mortgage on my house and the pre-selling of the book to subscribers more or less at cost. The remaining copies could not, I fondly imagined, fail to sell since this would surely be a work that no serious library or museum could fail to covet. As well as this innocent confidence in both myself and the curatorial world, I made one major monetary howler in my hasty additions: I omitted to count in any payment to myself in the costing of the enterprise. My finances have never wholly recovered from this naïve blunder, although by now all but a handful of copies have found a home.

Nonetheless there *was* a substantial group of trusting people willing to buy a book which, when money changed hands, merely consisted of unbound sheets of blank paper. Needless to say my great supporters Ruth and Marvin Sackner in Miami, whose celebrated archive of concrete and visual poetry houses so much of my work, were the first to subscribe to this pig in a poke; thus they and their children still have more copies of the *Inferno* between the five of them than they have refrigerators.

I was also fortunate in the team that I gathered together to make and print the work. The rare commitment of Nick Tite was augmented by that of Nick Hunter, who directed the lithography, and Chris Betambeau, who prepared the screenprints. Pella Erskine-Tulloch (the muse and *mia donna*

56.
Tom Phillips, *Inferno* XXXI:
King Kong

in the case) designed the definitive binding and, as a literal labour of love, devoted many hours to expertly typing out drafts of the translation. The typography was in the expert hands of Ian Mortimer, and Anthea Toorchen was the collator. Most of the pages of illustration were designed and printed in my studio where, as the project advanced, not an inch remained free of paper chaos. Silkscreening was done far away at Advanced Graphics, since I had become wary of its perilous chemicals.

As the translation ripened, I felt able to send my own clumsily typed drafts canto by canto to Frank Auerbach (himself an occasional translator and seasoned reader of poetry), who returned them with many suggestions for revision. Finally I showed the whole text to David Rudkin, who worked through it line by line with me during long patient sessions at my studio, or in his workroom, or most often in the lounge of the Randolph Hotel, Oxford, an old mutual haunt of our student days that lies halfway between us.

Nothing could have seemed more elitist than this extravagant three-volume set of the *Inferno*, which weighs in at over fourteen pounds. I was naturally keen to make it in some form more available and it was not long before, as has been the case with all my books, Hansjörg Mayer stepped in and produced in Stuttgart a handsome trade edition for Thames and Hudson.

57.
Tom Phillips, *Inferno*
XXXIV: Book of Light

go on; go on.

the heavens open
Look up; look up.

See the depth above us, and
endless space, and all
a ball of
milky lght
—the book of
stars
vibrating

and
two eternities
yet remain to be written.

This was not to be the end of the story. Seven years after the Talfourd Press book came out, Michael Kustow — now the Diaghilev of Channel 4 — had a wild idea. We had occasionally collaborated on many (and often doomed) projects since we first worked together as students in Oxford at the end of the fifties. He intimated that the channel might be interested in making a television version, extending my images into movement and getting actors to dramatize my translation. He suggested that I might work with a director then only known to an art-house coterie, Peter Greenaway. We made a pilot version of Canto V with myself playing all the parts except Francesca. Three years later we were at last allowed, thanks to the encouragement of Jeremy Isaacs, Channel 4's founding supremo, to start work on the whole of the *Inferno*. This was certainly at the time (and possibly still is) as ambitiously experimental as television has ever been. After eight cantos, each about ten minutes long, Channel 4 (now with its original cultural mission fading) decided, even though Peter and I had just been jointly awarded an Italia Prize, that this was enough of the polysemous and imbricated for even their most intellectually hardened viewer.

The end of the affair, although I did not know it then, was my journey to collect the prize at the Teatro Rossini in Pesaro. The ceremony, produced for television of course, ended with a Felliniesque scene in which I stumbled on to the stage and found myself to my amazement danced around by a bevy of near-naked girls towards a glittering compère in a silver suit. Amid balloons and lurid strobe-lighting I was urged with my scroll into a general swaying finale into whose confusing rock choreography I was inducted by yet more smiling Salomes. For all the euphoria, this, for the project, was a dance of death. What remains of the rest is the original recording to camera of the magically character-perfect voices of John Gielgud and Bob Peck, together with footage of a crowd of naked Dutch extras and some filmed fragments of commentary from the likes of David Rudkin and David Attenborough. Nonetheless being let loose on the exciting (if still almost unexplored) medium of television was one of the most exciting episodes of my life, just as making the original book, with its generous ration of Hershey Heaven, had been one of the most invigorating (Figs. 56, 57).

Further reading

Chapter 1

Barański, Zygmunt G., *'Chiosar con altro testo'. Leggere Dante nel Trecento* (Fiesole, 2001).

Bellomo, Saverio, *Dizionario dei commentatori danteschi* (Florence, 2004).

Gilson, Simon, *Dante and Renaissance Florence* (Cambridge, 2005).

Minnis, A. J. and A. B. Scott with the assistance of David Wallace, *Medieval Literary Theory and Criticism c. 1100–c. 1375* (Oxford, 1988).

Minnis, Alastair and Ian Johnson (eds.), *The Cambridge History of Literary Criticism*, ii: *The Middle Ages* (Cambridge, 2005), 561–611 (chapters by Zygmunt G. Barański and by Steven Botterill).

Chapter 2

Billanovich, Giuseppe, *Petrarca e il primo Umanesimo* (Padua, 1996).

Feo, Michele (ed.), *Petrarca nel tempo. Tradizione, lettori e immagini delle opere. Catalogo della mostra, Arezzo, Sottochiesa di San Francesco, 22 novembre 2003 – 27 gennaio 2004* (Pontedera, 2003).

Foster, Kenelm, *Petrarch: Humanist and Poet* (Edinburgh, 1984).

Hainsworth, Peter, *Petrarch the Poet. An Introduction to the 'Rerum vulgarium fragmenta'* (London, 1988).

Kraye, Jill (ed.), *The Cambridge Companion to Renaissance Humanism* (Cambridge, 1996).

Mann, Nicholas, *Petrarch* (Oxford, 1984).

Chapter 3

Branca, Vittore, *Boccaccio medievale e nuovi studi sul 'Decameron'* (6th edn, Florence, 1986).

Branca, Vittore (ed.), *Boccaccio visualizzato: Narrare per parole e per immagini fra medioevo e rinascimento*, 3 vols (Turin, 1999).

de la Mare, Albinia C., and Catherine Reynolds, 'Illustrated Boccaccio manuscripts in Oxford Libraries', *Studi sul Boccaccio*, 20 (1992), 45–72.

Kirkham, Victoria, *Fabulous Vernacular: Boccaccio's 'Filocolo' and the Art of Medieval Fiction* (Ann Arbor, 2001).

Rickets, Jill M., *Visualizing Boccaccio: Studies on Illustrations of the Decameron, from Giotto to Pasolini* (Cambridge, 1997).

Chapter 4

Bellomo, Saverio, 'La critica dantesca nel Cinquecento', in Enrico Malato (ed.), *Storia della letteratura italiana*, xi: *La critica letteraria dal Due al Novecento* (Rome, 2003), 311–23.

Dionisotti, Carlo, 'Dante nel Quattrocento', in *Atti del Congresso Internazionale di Studi Danteschi (20–27 aprile 1965)*, 2 vols (Florence, 1965–66), i. 333–78.

Gilson, Simon, *Dante and Renaissance Florence* (Cambridge, 2005).

Parker, Deborah, *Commentary and Ideology: Dante in the Renaissance* (Durham and London, 1993).

Richardson, Brian, 'Editing Dante's *Commedia*, 1472–1629', in Theodore J. Cachey Jr (ed.), *Dante Now: Current Trends in Dante Studies* (Notre Dame, 1995), 237–62.

Chapter 5

Brand, C. P., *Italy and the English Romantics. The Italianate Fashion in Early Nineteenth-century England* (Cambridge, 1957).

Dionisotti, Carlo, 'Varia fortuna di Dante', in *Geografia e storia della letteratura italiana* (Turin, 1967), 255–303.

Ellis, Steve, *Dante and English Poetry* (Cambridge, 1983).

Milbank, Alison, *Dante and the Victorians* (Manchester, 1998).

Pite, Ralph, *The Circle of Our Vision: Dante's Presence in English Romantic Poetry* (Oxford, 1994).

Toynbee, Paget, *Dante in English Literature from Chaucer to Cary (c. 1380–1844)*, 2 vols (London, 1909).

Toynbee, Paget, *Britain's Tribute to Dante in Literature and Art. A Chronological Record of 540 Years, c. 1380–1920* (London, 1921).

Chapter 6

Doughty, Oswald, *A Victorian Romantic: Dante Gabriel Rossetti* (Oxford, 1960).

Giannantonio, Pompeo, *Bibliografia di Gabriele Rossetti (1806–1958)* (Florence, 1959). This has been brought up-to-date by the bibliography in Gabriele Rossetti, *Poesie, ordinate da Giosuè Carducci*, ed. Mario Cimino (Lanciano, 2004), 41–66.

Oliva, Gianni (ed.), *I Rossetti tra Italia e Inghilterra* (Proceedings of the International Conference at Vasto, 1982) (Rome, 1984).

Oliva, Gianni (ed.), *Gabriele Rossetti a 150 anni dalla morte* (Proceedings of the International Conference at Vasto, 2004), in *Studi medievali e moderni*, 2 (Naples, 2004).

Surtees, Virginia, *The Paintings and Drawings of Dante Gabriel Rossetti 1828–1882: A Catalogue Raisonné*, 2 vols (Oxford, 1971).

Vincent, E. R., *Gabriele Rossetti in England* (Oxford, 1936).

Waller, R. D., *The Rossetti Family (1824–1854)* (Manchester, 1932).

Chapter 7

Ady, C. M., rev. Diego Zancani, 'Paget Jackson Toynbee', in *Oxford Dictionary of National Biography* (Oxford, 2004), lv, 188–89.

Braida, Antonella, *Dante and the Romantics* (Basingstoke, 2004).

A. Cippico, H. E. Goad, E. G. Gardner *et al.*, *Dante. Essays in Commemoration 1321–1921* (Oxford, 1921).

Milbank, Alison, *Dante and the Victorians* (Manchester, 1998).

Toynbee, Paget Jackson, *Dante Studies and Researches* (London, 1902).

Notes

Chapter 1

1. The quotations come, respectively, from: Philip H. Wicksteed and Edmund G. Gardner, *Dante and Giovanni del Virgilio* (London, 1902), 174; Graziolo Bambaglioli, *Commento all'"Inferno' di Dante*, ed. Luca Carlo Rossi (Pisa, 1998), 3; Guido da Pisa, *Expositiones et Glose Super Comediam Dantis*, ed. Vincenzo Cioffari (Albany, NY, 1974), 4. All translations in this chapter are my own.

2. Dante Alighieri, *La Commedia secondo l'antica vulgata*, ed. Giorgio Petrocchi, 4 vols (2nd edn, Florence, 1994).

3. Guido da Pisa, *Expositiones*, 30–31. The term 'new poet' is found at the very opening of Guido's commentary (p. 1).

4. Dante Alighieri, *Convivio*, ed. Franca Brambilla Ageno, 3 vols (Florence, 1995), IV.vi.5.

5. Franco Sacchetti, *Il Trecentonovelle*, ed. Valerio Marucci (Rome, 1996), *novelle* CXIV and CXV.

6. The most important sets of glosses are the so-called Anonymous Lombard (*c*.1325); the *Chiose selmiane* (before 1337), named after their editor, Francesco Selmi; the *Chiose ambrosiane* (*c*.1355), named after the Ambrosiana Library of Milan, which houses the sole manuscript; and the *Chiose filippine* (before 1370), whose designation comes from the Philippine order which founded the Biblioteca dei Girolamini in Naples that conserves the sole manuscript. Many other glosses await editing.

7. Oxford, Bodleian Library, MS. Canon. Misc. 449.

8. Benvenuto da Imola, *Comentum super Dantis Aldigherij Comoediam*, ed. Jacopo Filippo Lacaita, 5 vols (Florence, 1887), i, 8.

9. *Epistole, XIII*, ed. Giorgio Brugnoli, in Dante Alighieri, *Opere minori*, 2 vols (Milan and Naples, 1979–88), ii, 608.

10. The glosses have not been published. They are preserved in MS. Florence, Biblioteca Nazionale Centrale, II I 39. The reference to the *Epistle* is found at fol. 133r. See Luca Azzetta, 'Le chiose alla *Commedia* e altre questioni dantesche', *L'Alighieri*, 21 (2003), 5–75.

11. Filippo Villani, *Expositio seu comentum super 'Comedia' Dantis Allegherii*, ed. Saverio Bellomo (Florence, 1989), Prefatio 32, p. 38.

12. See the chapters by Martin McLaughlin and Simon Gilson for an assessment of Dante's humanist reception.

Chapter 2

13. A complete list of Petrarch manuscripts in Britain is given in Nicholas Mann, 'Petrarch manuscripts in the British Isles', *Italia medioevale e umanistica*, 18 (1975), 139–514. Petrarch

manuscripts continue to turn up; for a recent discovery see Nicholas Mann, '"O Deus, qualis epistola!": a new Petrarch letter', *Italia medioevale e umanistica*, 17 (1974), 207–43.

14. Oxford, Exeter College, MS. 186; Oxford, Bodleian Library, MS. Canon. Pat. Lat. 210.

15. The fullest biography is by Ugo Dotti, *Vita di Petrarca* (Bari and Rome, 1987). For a biography in English, see Ernest Hatch Wilkins, *Life of Petrarch* (Chicago and London, 1961); but see also Nicholas Mann, 'From laurel to fig: Petrarch and the structures of the self', *Proceedings of the British Academy*, 105 (2000), 17–42.

16. The manuscript, with this autograph note and a miniature by Simone Martini, is now in Milan, Biblioteca Ambrosiana, formerly A 79 inf., now SP 10 27: for a facsimile, see *Francisci Petrarcae Vergilianus Codex*, ed. Giovanni Galbiati (Milan, 1930). On Petrarch's manuscripts, see Michele Feo (ed.), *Petrarca nel tempo. Tradizione, lettori e immagini delle opere. Catalogo della mostra, Arezzo, Sottochiesa di San Francesco, 22 novembre 2003 – 27 gennaio 2004* (Pontedera, 2003), containing many reproductions.

17. For studies in English of the Italian poetry, see Kenelm Foster, *Petrarch: Humanist and Poet* (Edinburgh, 1984), and Peter Hainsworth, *Petrarch the Poet. An Introduction to the 'Rerum vulgarium fragmenta'* (London, 1988).

18. On Petrarch's humanism, see Nicholas Mann, *Petrarch* (Oxford, 1984); Giuseppe Mazzotta, *The Worlds of Petrarch* (Durham, NC, 1993); Jill Kraye (ed.), *The Cambridge Companion to Renaissance Humanism* (Cambridge, 1996). Particularly useful for what follows is Peter Burke, *The Renaissance Sense of the Past* (London, 1969).

19. Parts of the text were actually transcribed in Petrarch's own hand: the manuscript is now British Library, Harley MS. 2493. See Giuseppe Billanovich, 'Petrarch and the textual tradition of Livy', *Journal of the Warburg and Courtauld Institutes*, 14 (1951), 137–208. For Petrarch's discoveries of original manuscripts see also Mann, *Petrarch* (1984), and L. D. Reynolds and N. G. Wilson, *Scribes and Scholars: A Guide to the Transmission of Greek and Latin Literature* (3rd edn, Oxford, 1991).

20. Francesco Petrarca, *Le familiari*, ed. Vittorio Rossi and Umberto Bosco, 4 vols (Florence, 1933–42), ii, 58. All English translations in this chapter are my own.

21. Francesco Petrarca, *Rerum memorandarum libri*, ed. Giuseppe Billanovich (Florence, 1943), 19.

22. Francesco Petrarca, *Africa*, ed. Nicola Festa (Florence, 1926), 278.

23. On these terms see Theodor E. Mommsen, 'Petrarch's conception of the "Dark Ages"', *Speculum*, 17 (1942), 226–42, reproduced in his *Medieval and Renaissance Studies*, ed. Eugene F. Rice, Jr (Ithaca, NY, 1959), 106–29; Martin McLaughlin, 'Humanist concepts of renaissance and middle ages in the Tre and Quattrocento', *Renaissance Studies*, 2 (1988), 131–42.

24. Francesco Petrarca, *De viris illustribus*, ed. Guido Martellotti (Florence, 1964), 4.

25. Petrarca, *Le familiari*, iv, 99.

26. See Martin McLaughlin, 'Latin and vernacular from Dante to the age of Lorenzo (1321–c.1500)', in *The Cambridge History of Literary Criticism*, ii: *The Middle Ages*, ed. Alastair Minnis and Ian Johnson (Cambridge, 2005), 612–25.

27. Vatican City, Biblioteca Apostolica Vaticana, Vat. Lat. 3196.

28. Francesco Petrarca, *Trionfi, Rime estravaganti, Codice degli abbozzi*, ed. Vinicio Pacca and Laura Paolino (Milan, 1996), 889.

29. Ibid. 809–10.

30. Oxford, Exeter College, MS. 186. For the dating of the manuscript and its annotations, see Giuseppe Billanovich, 'Nella biblioteca del Petrarca. Un altro Svetonio del Petrarca (Oxford, Exeter College, 186)', *Italia medioevale e umanistica*, 3 (1960), 28–58.

31. For Petrarch's modelling of his life on Augustus, see Martin McLaughlin, 'Biography and Autobiography in the Italian Renaissance', in Peter France and William St Clair (eds.), *Mapping Lives: The Uses of Biography* (Oxford, 2002), 37–65.

32. A replica still stands in Piazza dei Signori.

33. Oxford, Bodleian Library, MS. Canon. Ital. 70.

34. For example, in Oxford, Bodleian Library, Auct. 2Q inf. 1.45 (Fig 18).

35. See Brian Richardson, *Print Culture in Renaissance Italy. The Editor and the Vernacular Text 1470–1600* (Cambridge, 1994), 48–51.

Chapter 3

36. Vittore Branca's explanation of the term whose use he cemented for the study of these images can be found in his seminal chapter, 'Prime interpretazioni visuali del *Decameron*', in *Boccaccio medievale e nuovi studi sul 'Decameron'* (6th edn, Florence, 1986), 395–432.

37. Jill M. Rickets, *Visualizing Boccaccio: Studies on Illustrations of the Decameron, from Giotto to Pasolini* (Cambridge, 1997).

38. Vittore Branca (ed.), *Boccaccio visualizzato: Narrare per parole e per immagini fra medioevo e rinascimento*, 3 vols (Turin, 1999). Much of the material in this work first appeared in various issues of *Studi sul Boccaccio*, 15– (1985–), which is more widely available than the book.

39. Berlin, Staatsbibliothek der Stiftung Preussischer Kulturbesitz, MS. Hamilton 90.

40. Oxford, Bodleian Library, MS. Canon. Misc. 58.

41. A manuscript of Boccaccio's *Fiammetta* (Oxford, Bodleian Library, MS. Add. C. 25), probably written and decorated within the Montefeltro court at Urbino *c.* 1470, shows a typical decorative border and an empty shield in the lower margin, but contains no miniature.

42. Several of these can be seen in the British Library, where Harley MS. 1766 (Lydgate's translation) has 135 miniatures.

43. Middle Templar William Burdett eventually donated it to the library before or at the time of his death in 1608, when Bodley reported his legacy of thirty-six manuscripts to the Vice Chancellor.

44. Florence, Biblioteca Medicео-Laurenziana, MS. 52.9.

45. Albinia C. de la Mare and Catherine Reynolds, 'Illustrated Boccaccio manuscripts in Oxford Libraries', *Studi sul Boccaccio*, 20 (1992), 45–72. This invaluable article is included in Italian in *Boccaccio visualizzato* (n.38 above).

46. He uses the term widely in his writing, but chiefly in the article cited in n.36.

47. Paris, Bibliothèque nationale de France, MSS. It. 482 and It. 63, dating from *c.* 1370 and 1427, respectively.

48. Oxford, Bodleian Library, MS. Holkham misc. 49, bought by Thomas Coke, the first Earl, while travelling in Italy early in the eighteenth century; it was accepted by the state in lieu of inheritance tax and allocated to the Bodleian in 1981. The Bodleian's densely illustrated copy of Dante's *Commedia*, MS. Holkham misc. 48, is from the same source.

49. Oxford, Bodleian Library, MS. Canon. Ital. 85.

50. See *Boccaccio visualizzato*, ii, 297–301.

51. See 'The Poisoned Peacock', in Victoria Kirkham, *Fabulous Vernacular: Boccaccio's 'Filocolo' and the Art of Medieval Fiction* (Ann Arbor, 2001), 200–50.

52. This is examined in detail by Gianvittorio Dillon in 'I primi incunaboli illustrati e il *Decameron* veneziano del 1492', in Branca, *Boccaccio visualizzato*, iii, 291–318.

53. Oxford, Bodleian Library, Douce 287.

54. Oxford, Bodleian Library, Arch. G. c.26.

55. Oxford, Bodleian Library, Douce 216 and 215.

56. Oxford, Bodleian Library, S. Seld. c. 2(1).

57. Oxford, Bodleian Library, Toynbee 3531.

58. Oxford, Bodleian Library, Fic. 2742 d.20/2.

Chapter 4

59. For fuller documentation of these traditions, see my *Dante and Renaissance Florence* (Cambridge, 2005). The quotation is from Bonaccorso da Montemagno, preface to his *Cammino di Dante*, ed. G. Bruschi, in 'Ser Piero Bonaccorsi e il suo *Cammino di Dante*', *Il Propugnatore*, 4 (1891), 2 vols, ii, 308-48 (p. 309). All translations from Italian and Latin are mine.

60. Guido da Pisa, *Expositiones et Glose super Comediam Dantis*, ed. Vincenzo Cioffari (Albany, NY,

1974), 4. The idea of Dante presiding over a cultural rebirth is stressed by, among others, Boccaccio, Filippo Villani, Gianozzo Manetti, and Cristoforo Landino.

61. Antonio Lanza, 'Invectiva contra a certi caluniatori di Dante, del Petrarca e del Boccaccio', in *Polemiche e berte letterarie nella Firenze del primo Quattrocento* (Rome, 1971), 261–67.

62. *Epistolario di Coluccio Salutati*, ed. Francesco Novati, 4 vols (Rome, 1891–1911), iv, 161.

63. Interest in measuring the structure and site of Dante's Hell is found in sixteenth-century commentaries on the *Commedia*, independent treatises, and lectures – most famously the two delivered by Galileo Galilei before the Florentine Academy in the late 1580s.

64. *Comento sopra la Comedia*, ed. Paolo Procaccioli, 4 vols (Rome, 2001), i, 221.

65. Ibid. 266.

66. Pietro Bembo, *Prose della volgar lingua*, in Carlo Dionisotti (ed.), *Prose e rime* (Turin, 1960), 178.

67. *De vulgari eloquentia* was re-discovered by Giovan Giorgio Trissino (1478–1550) in the 1520s. Trissino printed his own vernacular version (1529) at the presses of Tolomeo Janiculo (i.e. Bartolomeo Zanetti) in Vicenza; the first Latin edition was printed in Paris (1577) by Jacopo Corbinelli (1535–90).

68. See Davide Dalmas, *Dante nella crisi religiosa del Cinquecento italiano: da Trifon Gabriele a Lodovico Castelvetro* (Rome, 2005).

Chapter 5

69. Paget Toynbee, *Dante in English Literature from Chaucer to Cary (c. 1380–1844)*, 2 vols (London, 1909). Toynbee's own contribution is the subject of Chapter 7.

70. T. S. Eliot, 'What Dante means to me', in *To Criticize the Critic* (London, 1965), 132.

71. Percy Bysshe Shelley, 'Defence of Poetry', in *The Major Works* (Oxford, 2003), 701.

72. See Paul Bénichou, *Romantismes français*, 2 vols (Paris, 1996), ii, 1487–2017.

73. Silvio Pellico, *Francesca da Rimini*, act 3, scene 2 (Paris, 1848), 490. The translations from this play are my own.

74. C. P. Brand, *Italy and the English Romantics: The Italianate Fashion in Early Nineteenth-century England* (Cambridge, 1957), 71.

75. Michael Pitwood, *Dante and the French Romantics* (Geneva, 1985), 266–67.

76. For a fuller idea of Francesca's frequent appearances in the cultural output of the nineteenth century, see A. H. Mathew, *Francesca da Rimini in Legend and History* (London, 1908).

77. See Claudio Poppi (ed.), *Sventurati Amanti: Il mito di Paolo e Francesca nell'800* (Milan, 1994).

78. Pellico, *Francesca da Rimini*, act 1, scene 5.

79. Antonio Gallergo, *Italy, Past and Present*, 2 vols (London, 1848), ii, 170.

80. Adam Smith, 'The theory of moral sentiment', in *Adam Smith's Moral and Political Philosophy*, ed. Herbert W. Schneider (New York, 1970), 73–74.

81. Edmund Burke, letter to an unknown recipient in *The Correspondence of Edmund Burke*, ed. Thomas W. Copeland *et al.*, 10 vols (Cambridge, 1958–78), vi, 78–81. For an extended study of Rousseau's 'sentimental' influence on Robespierre, see Gregory Dart, *Rousseau, Robespierre and the French Revolution* (Cambridge, 1999).

82. For a discussion of Austen, sensibility, and sociability, see Gillian Russell and Clara Tuite (eds.), *Romantic Sociability: Social Networks and Literary Culture in Britain 1770–1840* (Cambridge, 2002), 8–9; and also Clara Tuite, *Romantic Austen: Sexual Politics and the Literary Canon* (Cambridge, 2002).

83. Thomas Love Peacock, *Nightmare Abbey*, in *The Novels of Thomas Love Peacock*, ed. David Garnett, 2 vols (London, 1963), i, 379–80.

84. John Keats, letter 123 to George and Georgiana Keats, 16 April 1819, in *The Letters of John Keats*, ed. Maurice Buxton Forman (2nd edn, London, 1935), 326.

85. William Hazlitt, *The Collected Works of William Hazlitt*, 12 vols (London, 1902), ix, 252.

86. For a discussion of Hazlitt's hybrid, literary-cum-conversational prose-style, see Tom Paulin, *The Day-Star of Liberty: William Hazlitt's Radical Style* (London, 1998), 271–97.

87. Francesco de Sanctis, *De Sanctis on Dante*, essays ed. and transl. by Joseph Rossi and Alfred Galpin (Madison, 1957), 40.

88. Ibid. 40.

89. Letter to Modest Tchaikovsky, 14 October 1876, quoted in Alexander Poznansky, *Tchaikovsky* (London, 1993), 190.

90. Alison Milbank's excellent study, *Dante and the Victorians* (Manchester, 1998), amply demonstrates the extent of Dante's popularity and of his influence after 1830, not least in relation to John Ruskin's aesthetic thought. It seems more important to observe that the tenor of Dante allusions changed following a change in the political landscape.

91. Gabriele D'Annunzio, *Francesca da Rimini* (Milan, 1902). The volume was dedicated to the actress who played Francesca, Eleanora Duse.

92. Gabriele D'Annunzio, *Francesca da Rimini*, trans. Arthur Symons (London, 1902), xiv.

93. Quoted in Milbank, *Dante and the Victorians*, 150.

Chapter 6

94. Modern scholarship recognizes *Vita nova* as the correct spelling, and it is used thus in the essays in this volume. However, the notes to this chapter use the spelling given on the title-page of the edition cited, e.g. *Vita nuova*.

95. Gabriele's other academies included the Ardenti of Viterbo, the Orezia of Palermo, and the Società Pontaniana of Naples. Proud of his academic affiliations, he includes these honours in his versified autobiography (see n.96).

96. Gabriele Rossetti, *La vita mia. Il testamento*, ed. Gianni Oliva (Lanciano, 2004), 114.

97. 'Poetry was the root of both my literary fame and also of my downfall. [...] The King, seeing me so revered by the public, and fearing that I could influence them, began to feel a mortal hatred for me, and wanted to have me in his power.' Gabriele Rossetti, *Carteggi*, ed. Tobia R. Toscano, Sergio Minichini, Alfonso Caprio, Philip Horne and John Woodhouse, 6 vols (Naples, 1984–2006), contains many autobiographical reminiscences, including this wonderfully spontaneous letter to Charles Lyell, dated 2 June 1840 (iv, 365).

98. John Hookham Frere had been English Ambassador to Spain; he later provided Rossetti with support and references for his sojourn in London, and later still, along with Charles Lyell of Kinnordy, gave considerable financial subsidies for Rossetti's Dante publications.

99. Its precise date of composition is uncertain; it was collected in several posthumous anthologies before being published on its own by Barbera (Florence, 1862). Carducci included it in his anthology; see n.100.

100. Gabriele Rossetti, *Poesie, ordinate da Giosuè Carducci*, ed. Mario Cimini (Lanciano, 2004), 165–66.

101. Gabriele Rossetti, *Carteggi*, i, 132, letter of 20 July 1824; see ibid. 145 (to Dora Moore) and 153 (to Susan Frere).

102. Ibid. 181, letter from Cary dated 26 January 1825 concerning Rossetti's new volume, *La Divina Commedia di Dante Alighieri, con comento analitico di Gabriele Rossettti in sei volumi*, 2 vols (London, 1826–27), henceforth *Comento analitico*.

103. In the *Quarterly Review* of January 1828, 57–59, in an anonymous review of Thomas McCrie's *History of the Reformation in Italy*, the Reverend John James Blunt, future Lady Margaret Professor of Theology in Cambridge, while complimenting Rossetti on his erudition, made witty parenthetical remarks concerning the 'strange fantasies' he had recently encountered in Rossetti's *Comento analitico*. Rossetti, apoplectic with rage and resentment, discovered who the perpetrator was and wrote to complain. Rossetti's letter of January 1828, and Blunt's calm letter of explanation to him, are published in *Carteggi*, ii, 95 and 173.

104. Ugo Foscolo, *Discorso sul testo della Divina Commedia di Dante* (London, 1825), p. CL; available in Ugo Foscolo, *Saggi critici*, ed. Enzo Bottasso (2nd edn, Turin, 1962), 276. Interestingly, Foscolo pre-dated his actual 1826 publication, while Rossetti's *Comento* (actually 1825) was post-dated 1826.

105. 'Discorso preliminare', in *Comento analitico* i, p. lxvi.

106. Elaborated by Rossetti in his *Disamina del sistema allegorico*, in *Comento analitico*, i, 378–79.

107. Rossetti's inclusion of such writers as Milton and Bunyan amongst his cryptographic

authors added much to the puzzlement of Charles Lyell.

108. Antonio Panizzi, *Osservazioni sul Comento analitico* (Florence, 1832), 24. The anonymous review was first published in *The Foreign Review*, 2 (October 1828), 175–95.

109. Mario Praz, *Il patto col serpente* (3rd edn, Milan, 1973), 141. Praz, following the defensive opinions of Pompeo Giannantonio, wrongly implied that Rossetti's British patrons encouraged his delusions. This was not true. Rossetti stubbornly ignored their criticisms, steamrollering through his crazier ideas despite their incredulity or declared incomprehension.

110. All published in London.

111. Gabriele Rossetti, *Comento analitico al Purgatorio di Dante Alighieri*, ed. Pompeo Giannantonio (Florence, 1966–67).

112. Gabriele Rossetti, *Carteggi*, ii, 252: 'In order to remind myself of the painful period during which I have been commenting on [Dante] in exile, I will renew his name in my family. Just a few days ago my wife gave birth to a little Rossetti. I will call him Dante' (letter of 28 May 1828).

113. There are many editions of the *Vita nova*, and most texts are uncontroversial. The best volume for a study of Dante Gabriel's translation and illustration is the bilingual edition which also includes all the Rossetti illustrations published together for the first time: Dante Gabriel Rossetti, *Vita nuova*, ed. Corrado Gizzi (Milan, 1983). For easy accessibility, quotations here are from the Everyman edition with an introduction by Edmund Gardner: Dante Gabriel Rossetti, *Poems, Early Italian Poets, and Dante and his Circle* (London, 1915). *New Life* is at 217–310, this quotation at 301. The painting concerned is in the collection of the Ashmolean Museum, Oxford.

114. Rossetti, *Poems*, 271–72. This painting, too, is in the Ashmolean collection.

115. Ibid. 305.

116. Dante Gabriel Rossetti, *The House of Life* (composed at various intervals), available in *D. G. Rossetti's Poetical Works: A New Edition in One Volume*, ed. W. M. Rossetti (London, 1895), 176–227. For Robert Buchanan's dastardly, if sociologically hilarious, review, see his *The Fleshly School of Poetry* (London, 1872), published by Buchanan deliberately hiding under the pseudonym 'Thomas Maitland'.

Chapter 7

117. Oxford, Bodleian Library, MS. Toynbee d. 23, fol. 20. The postcard was sent from Ko-ya-san, Yamato.

118. Paget Toynbee, *Specimens of Old French, ix-xv Centuries, with Introduction, Notes, and Glossary* (Oxford, 1892).

119. August Brachet, *A Historical Grammar of the French Language, from the French, Rewritten and Enlarged by P. Toynbee* (Oxford, 1896).

120. Paget Toynbee, *A Dictionary of Proper Names and Notable Matters in the Works of Dante*, rev. Charles Singleton (Oxford, 1968).

121. *Supplement to the Letters of Horace Walpole, Fourth Earl of Orford, Chronologically Arranged and Edited with Notes and Indices by Paget Toynbee* (Oxford, 1918–25).

122. Dante Alighieri, *Tutte le opere di Dante Alighieri, nuovamente rivedute nel testo da Edward Moore* (Oxford, 1894). Toynbee also published an *Index of Proper Names in the Prose Works and Canzoniere of Dante* (Boston, 1894). The *Enciclopedia Dantesca*, 6 vols (Rome, 1984), iii, 1025, refers to Moore's 'Oxford Dante' as 'an important link in the evolution of studies on Dante's texts'.

123. Paget Toynbee, 'Oxford and Dante', in *Dante. Essays in Commemoration 1321–1921* (London, 1921), 56.

124. *Comments of John Ruskin on the 'Divina Commedia'*, ed. George P. Huntington (Boston, 1903), 3. See also Hilary Fraser, 'Ruskin, Italy, and the past', in *Britain and Italy: From Romanticism to Modernism*, ed. Martin McLaughlin (Oxford, 2000), 87–106.

125. Toynbee, 'Oxford and Dante', 57.

126. Oxford, Bodleian Library, MS. Toynbee, d. 21, fol. 429.

127. The London booksellers were: Brown, Bull & Auvache, Dobell, Edwards, Hankinson,

Hodgsons, Isaacs, Leighton, Maggs, McCaskie, Nutt, Quaritch, Reader, Rimell, Sotheby's, Sotheran, Thorp, Tregaskis, Voynich, Winter, Wright & Jones.

128. Item by S. G. in the 'Notes & News' section, *Bodleian Quarterly Record*, 4 (1923–25), 74–75. See also 'Portraits of Dante', *Bodleian Quarterly Record*, 2 (1917–19), 55–57; 'Documents and Records', ibid., 204–5, and F. M.'s note on Toynbee's death, *Bodleian Quarterly Record*, 7 (1932–34), 50. In 1909 a *Report of the Curators of the Taylor Institution for the Year 1909* indicates that 'A large and valuable collection of books was presented to the Institution by Dr Paget Toynbee to form the nucleus of a Seminar Library for students reading for the Final Honours School in French'. Many of these, with the Toynbee *ex-libris*, have survived in the Taylorian Library.

129. Catalogued in Mary Clapinson and T. D. Rogers, *Summary Catalogue of Post-Medieval Western Manuscripts in the Bodleian Library* 3 vols (Oxford, 1991), ii, 1351–55.

130. Bodleian Library, MS. Toynbee d. 25, fol. 25, letter dated 13 June 1913.

131. The decree of thanks mentions 'about eight hundred choice volumes, printed and manuscript, chiefly relating to Petrarch, Boccaccio, and Italian literature generally, together with papers relating to Horace Walpole and the Strawberry Hill Press, and Japanese illustrated works'. Oxford, Bodleian Library, MS. Toynbee d. 25, fol. 33.

132. No. 1677 of part V of *Bibliotheca Sussexiana* sold in 1845. This copy cost £6, and was bought from Maggs in London in 1898.

133. Now Oxford, Balliol College Library, 3.a.1. The other copy is in the Bodleian, Toynbee 1107 c.

134. Oxford, Balliol College Library, 3.a.17.

135. Further information on the collection is in Diego Zancani, 'Una biblioteca di cent'anni fa: la "Dante Collection" di Paget Toynbee (1855–1932)', in *Anatomie bibliologiche. Saggi di storia del libro per il centenario de 'La Bibliofilia'* (Florence, 1999), 495–512.

136. Cyril Bayley, tutor in Classics and Balliol Fellow Librarian, wrote to Toynbee (17 June 1913): 'We are grateful to you for consulting us in this matter and, I need not add, for all that you have done & intend to do for the College Library' (Oxford, Bodleian Library, MS. Toynbee d. 25, fol. 31). Some information concerning the Toynbee bequest to Balliol is contained in the Balliol College Archives (MBP 322), but I have been unable to find a list of the books which actually entered the College library.

137. Bodley 2386-15-18. Another volume of *Articles on Dante and Boccaccio* was bequeathed to Balliol College, shelfmark 195 a 9.

138. Oxford, Bodleian Library, Toynbee 3551*–3551**.

139. For the importance of this edition, edited by Pietro Bembo, see Simon Gilson, Chapter 4. Another gift from Butler, a copy of *Amoroso Convivio* (Venice: Zuane Antonio e Fradelli da Sabio, 1521), was received in 1898.

140. In Butler's obituary, published anonymously in *The Times*, 28 February 1910, his ability in writing notes to the *Divine Comedy* is criticized partly because 'he was not equipped with a sufficient knowledge of the Tuscan language'. The obituary, though written by the editor of *The Times*, was based on 'data partly supplied' by W. W. Vernon. The latter wrote to Toynbee on 28 February 1910 that when the *Times* Editor had asked him to write an 'appreciatory note' of Butler's Dante works, 'I told him that it was not possible for me to do that, as I had nearly always been in controversy with him on his interpretation of Italian, but I wrote him a private letter (by hand) in which I said all that I could honestly say in praise of the poor man. I have had a letter from the Editor this morning with warm thanks, and his obituary notice *contains* all that I had written' (Oxford, Bodleian Library, MS. Toynbee d. 24, fol. 133).

141. On 21 March 1906 Charles Shadwell wrote to Toynbee that he was busy moving into a new house: 'As you may suppose, I have very little time for Dante, and I am not yet half way through the 7th canto of *Paradiso*: it is the most difficult, and I think the least interesting of all that I have yet encountered' (Oxford, Bodleian Library, MS. Toynbee d. 24, fols. 47–48).

142. Paget Toynbee, *In the Footprints of Dante* (London, 1907).

143. Paget Toynbee, 'Sollenare', *Bulletin Italien*, 4.3 (1904), 181–85.

144. A detailed account of the Society's activities, and a list of its members, was published by Toynbee 'in view of the approaching celebration of the sixth centenary of the death of Dante', in *The Oxford Dante Society. A Record of Forty-four Years (1876–1920)*, compiled by Paget Toynbee (Oxford, 1920).

145. See Antonella Braida, *Dante and the Romantics* (Basingstoke, 2004), and Alison Milbank, *Dante and the Victorians* (Manchester, 1998), 17–25.

146. Toynbee, 'Oxford and Dante', 59–60.

147. John Morley mentions Panizzi's influence in his biography of Gladstone: *The Life of William Ewart Gladstone*, 3 vols (London, 1903), i, 389. In 1868 Panizzi became a Senator of the Kingdom of Italy and in 1869 he was made KCB by Queen Victoria.

148. Quoted in Toynbee, 'Oxford and Dante', 60.

149. See David Wallace, 'Dante in English', in *The Cambridge Companion to Dante*, ed. Rachel Jacoff (Cambridge, 1993), 237–58, and chapter 6 of this volume.

150. *The Divine Comedy, Translated in terza rima by John Dayman* (London, 1865) and *The 'Divina Commedia' of Dante, Translated into English Verse by James Ford* (London, 1870).

151. Oxford, Bodleian Library, MS. Toynbee e. 6, fol. 26 (in a *post scriptum* to a letter of 10 October [1913]).

152. Paget Toynbee, *Dante Alighieri: His Life and Works*, rev. and enlarged (London, 1910), 114–17. In a letter to Guido Biagi, dated 29 September 1921, Toynbee wrote: 'My physical condition unfits me to travel, otherwise I would have liked to be at Ravenna on Sept. 13–4 and to have seen the pageant at Florence.' But he was also critical of recent publications completed probably in a rush for the centenary: 'I have been reading the new text of the "Opere di Dante", & am gradually working my way through it. There are some astonishing things in it, which I do not feel able to accept, & some of which I cannot help thinking will not find a place in the final edition – at any rate, I devoutly hope so. Of course, the fact that the scope of the present volume does not admit of an "apparatus criticus" & notes, places both editors and critics in a somewhat false position. However, it is a great satisfaction to have this volume as the first fruits of all the labour that has been expended, & no doubt it will benefit by the rigorous criticism which it is sure to receive from many quarters.' (Florence, Biblioteca Nazionale Centrale, Carteggi: Biagi, 7, 65).

153. *Le Opere di Dante.* Testo critico della Società Dantesca Italiana (Florence, 1921). In the copy of this book bequeathed by Paget Toynbee to Balliol College, there is a letter by the editor of *The Times*, dated 3 August 1921, asking him to write a review, which appeared in the *Times Literary Supplement* of 14 September 1921, in an issue 'in honour of Dante'.

154. *Oxford Dictionary of National Biography* (Oxford, 2004), lv, 189.

155. A postcard by M. Barbi, dated 1 July [1921], mentions that a copy of the *Opere di Dante* which had been in print for over a month was delayed because of the binding, but it would be sent to Toynbee 'on behalf of all the contributors'.

156. *Dantis Alagherii Epistolae. The Letters of Dante. Emended Text with Introduction, Translation, Notes and Indices and Appendix on the Cursus by Paget Toynbee* (Oxford, 1920).

Chapter 8

157. These notes augment and extend the account given in Tom Phillips, *Works and Texts to 1992* (London, 1992), 219–47.

158. Originally drafted by Tom Phillips in 1986 as the end couplet of 'Curriculum Vitae XIX', these became the closing lines of 'Song of Myself', designed by the artist as a wire sculpture (exhibited at the Royal Academy in 2006). The whole text, a fanciful alliterative autobiography, was later set by Harrison Birtwistle in 1997 for baritone and viola. Birtwistle reworked it in 2006 for baritone, double bass, and percussion, to be performed at a concert forming the finale of Tom Phillips's Slade Lectures at Oxford University, which was given at the Holywell Music Room, Oxford. The work in this latter form is published by Boosey & Hawkes.